No King but God

No King but God

Walking as Jesus Walked

MICHAEL MANNING

RESOURCE *Publications* • Eugene, Oregon

NO KING BUT GOD
Walking as Jesus Walked

Resource Publications
An Imprint of Wipf and Stock Publishers
199 W. 8th Ave., Suite 3
Eugene, OR 97401

www.wipfandstock.com

ISBN 13: 978-1-4982-3150-3

Manufactured in the U.S.A.

For all those who pass through Graih's doors.
We are in the process of becoming a people.
Be touched by God.
Kyrie, eleison.

Contents

Acknowledgments

In many ways this book is not my own. No-one stands alone. My heartfelt thanks go to all those who generously read the drafts of the chapters and offered clarification, criticism, and insight. Your grace and kindness were encouraging and the lack of clarity in what follows remains my own!

More thanks than I can give go also: to Matthew Wimer and all those at Wipf and Stock, for taking this project on and their help throughout; to all who pass through the doors of Hilary Road, who constantly broaden my horizons; to Phil Craine, the most graceful man I know; to Arthur Williams, Gordon Buist, and all at Stauros for constant encouragement, support, and wisdom; to Pat Clague, for gentle and unfailing wisdom; to Bill Platt, for being a friend beyond praise, may your sojourning lead you closer to Jesus; to Jayne Platt, for so much fellow-service and support at Graih and beyond; to Kenny and Carol Best, for modeling the radical hospitality and generosity of God in so many ways; to David Gordon, for a generous stream of theological stimulation in books and conversations; to David Smith, for wisdom and encouragement at just the right time; to the church at Broadway Baptist, for being my family; to my parents and sisters, for always encouraging my writing and the strange paths I have walked, your love has helped make me who I am; to Elan, whose wisdom, grace, and love has marked and transformed me more than I can tell; to Aedan and Cian, for the love and the challenge and the joy.

Acknowledgments

And to all those who have passed through Graih's doors. You have shaped me more than I have shaped you. This book is for you. May the kingdom come.

To the glory of God.

Introduction

No King but God

O sing to the LORD a new song;
sing to the LORD, all the earth.
Sing to the LORD, bless his name;
tell of his salvation from day to day.
Declare his glory among the nations,
his marvellous works among all the peoples.
For great is the LORD, and greatly to be praised;
he is to be revered above all gods.
For all the gods of the peoples are idols,
but the LORD made the heavens.
Honour and majesty are before him;
strength and beauty are in his sanctuary.
Ascribe to the LORD, O families of the peoples,
ascribe to the LORD glory and strength.
Ascribe to the LORD the glory due his name;
bring an offering, and come into his courts.
Worship the LORD in holy splendour;
tremble before him, all the earth.

Say among the nations, 'The LORD is king!
The world is firmly established; it shall never be moved.

> He will judge the peoples with equity.
> Let the heavens be glad, and let the earth rejoice;
> let the sea roar, and all that fills it;
> let the field exult, and everything in it.
> Then shall all the trees of the forest sing for joy
> before the LORD; for he is coming,
> for he is coming to judge the earth.
> He will judge the world with righteousness,
> and the peoples with his truth.
>
> —PSALM 96

"NO KING BUT GOD!" was the cry that echoed with revolutionary fervor around the tumultuous land of Palestine in the century or so either side of Jesus' birth. Zealous Jews knew that YHWH was God. They knew that one day he was going to vindicate his people. They uttered this cry as a prayer, as a challenge, as a shout of battle, and as an encouragement. Above all it was a hope and a longing that consumed them. Faced with the oppression of Rome without and the compromise and collusion of other Jews within various groups offered their answer. Some sided with the despised pagan overlords to keep religious, political, and economic power. Some withdrew to the desert to embody a community of purity and wait for their vindication. Some urged fellow-Jews to keep Torah rightly, in anticipation of and participation in YHWH's coming. Some took up the sword against Romans and fellow-Jews and waged the holy war by which YHWH's kingdom would break in. No King but God.[1]

Into this political, social, economic, and religious maelstrom there was another voice. Another prophet telling the ancient Exodus stories of redemption, calling on people to turn around because YHWH's kingdom was near. His claims clashed with the

1. On the historical and theological background of the first century see Wright, *New Testament and People; Jesus and Victory; Resurrection of the Son; Paul and Faithfulness.* See also Horsley, *Jesus and Empire; Paul and Empire.*

others on offer and made him popular in some quarters, hated in others. As with all would-be revolutionary leaders at the time, he was crucified. This is what Rome did to those who opposed her. Another claim about YHWH's kingdom was crushed by the empire. The prophet was wrong.

Except that within a very short space of time, in lands far from Palestine, followers of this prophet were hauled before magistrates for "turning the world upside down." And the accusation against them? They claimed there was another king, apart from Caesar. His name was Jesus (Acts 17:7).

The heartfelt, aching longing expressed in the cry "No King but God" found powerful redefinition in the early church. They would have recognized and affirmed that longing even as they re-thought the very concepts of "king" and "God" around Jesus. There was no King but God, but Jesus looked very different from the gods and kings that so many imagined, worshiped, and followed. The claims of this new King likewise transformed every aspect of life: political, social, economic, and religious (although the ancient world knew nothing of such compartmentalized and truncated spheres of life). Something amazing had happened. The world had changed forever.

Psalm 96 stands in just this stream of longing for YHWH's kingdom. In a ruptured world the claims of God stand not just as claims *for* something but also *against* something. Throughout scripture we see God and his people naming, confronting, diminishing, and overthrowing the "idols of the nations." Anything that distorts or demeans God's good creation must be dealt with. Too often we set up the works of our own hands to worship. The idolatrous urge of humanity must be challenged. We become what we adore. The pain and oppression of a groaning people and a groaning creation must be judged, not in a condemnatory sense but in the joy that such a judgment of righteousness and truth and equity will bring. There remain many idols today and Psalm 96 is programmatic for the rest of this book. We will look at five contemporary idols—faith, freedom, the state, wealth, and the individual—and in each case we will see how they are challenged as God becomes King.

As we consider various areas of life we should remember that they are not discrete. We are not so much examining half a dozen separate areas as we are looking at a whole from many angles. All of these areas interact with and cohere with the others. They all contribute towards an expression of life where there is no King but God. This is by no means a complete examination of such a life, merely an attempt to indicate what may be involved. The cry remains a longing, but it is a longing fraught with questions and uncertainties rather than clear answers. At the same time, we walk, or stumble, on a path that may be narrow but has been walked before. There is one who goes with us, and we need not be afraid. I had intended to subtitle the book "a prophetic-utopian manifesto for the liberated life" but the image of walking, rooted in both activity and direction, has impressed itself upon me in the writing (quite apart from the initial subtitle being a technical mouthful!). This is about how we live and where we are headed. It remains, however, a work longing for liberation, in the belief that the clearer view we have of the good (the utopia) the better we can discern how God's kingdom might be lived out in the present (the prophetic). This embodiment of prophetic living and truth is always in opposition to a world and a church awash with idols, but there is a liberation. The longing of "No King but God" is very much a yearning and a prayer for my own life.

It will become apparent that the context in which we live and move and have our being is of immense importance, so a brief word on my own context. I have lived most of my life on the Isle of Man. My faith has been shaped in the Baptist tradition (in both agreement and disagreement!) in which I still stand. The island has many similarities with the UK but there are some important differences. The stretch of water engenders a sense of separation from the UK that leads to both backwater isolation and the freedom to do things differently. The fact that the island has its own government is a case in point. We inhabit a different political framework from the UK that brings independence, yet the febrile politics of small communities easily lead to corruption and inertia. This plays itself out in many areas of life, where the fact of a small society means that it is difficult for new ideas to gain traction. The (dis) economies of scale often lead to the maintenance of the status quo, as minority views on an island can sometimes be just a handful of individuals easily ignored. Change can be difficult. At the same time, when change does occur it can happen with astonishing speed and affect a far larger part of society than can happen in larger polities. On a small island small actions can lead very quickly to big differences, so the potential for wide-reaching change is great. The island's society has been powerfully influenced by the offshore financial sector for the past few decades, an area that we will consider in a later chapter. We have many of the same social problems as the UK, but on an island scale. This means that problems are often more hidden, denied, or avoided than recognized, uncovered, and addressed. The lack of plurality in the media and civic society can have a deadening effect on debate.

Perhaps the greatest influence on me, and my defining context, has been my involvement with Graih.[2] Graih is the Manx word for love and it is a charity that has pioneered services to those who are homeless or in insecure accommodation on the island. In this it has sought to bring to light some forgotten areas of Manx life and to at least attempt a response. The men and women I have met and have had the privilege of building relationships with through Graih have been a theological furnace that has fired my life and faith. Their stories and lives, often unheard and unseen on the margins of society, have spoken truth to me and challenged every area of my life. Many of their stories appear in the following pages, although names have been changed. We will look at the importance of the poor embodying truth and challenging us in a later chapter.

In these two contexts—the Isle of Man and Graih—this is a book written from the margins. In such contexts we can often

2. www.graih.org.im

glimpse things that the mainstream misses. The liminal—the marginal and those on the edge—have a prophetic perspective. If there is even a hint in the following pages of what life in the kingdom of God might look like then part of my longing will have been answered.

There is no King but God.

Chapter 1

The God of Obedience and the Idol of Faith

> He has told you, O mortal, what is good; and what does the LORD require of you but to do justice, and to love kindness, and to walk humbly with your God?
>
> —Micah 6:8

> Now by this we may be sure that we know him, if we obey his commandments. Whoever says, 'I have come to know him', but does not obey his commandments, is a liar, and in such a person the truth does not exist; but whoever obeys his word, truly in this person the love of God has reached perfection. By this we may be sure that we are in him: whoever says, 'I abide in him', ought to walk just as he walked.
>
> —1 John 2:3–6

JOHN, AS AN OLD man writing to his beloved children, is in no doubt about what lies at the heart of the Christian life. "You must walk as Jesus walked", he urges them. John, when pressed, goes straight to action as the determinant of whether one follows Jesus or not. It's not about belief, or statements of "knowledge" about

Jesus. What matters is what you do. Which way you walk. Who you follow.

John has just opened his letter writing about the word of life, about fellowship, about joy. In the verses immediately preceding those quoted above he talks about Jesus being the atoning sacrifice for our sins. And not only ours, but the sins of the whole world. He will go on to write what is arguably the greatest chapter on love in the scriptural canon, tying it expressly to practical love shown to one another.

The heart of these verses, and the heart of this book, points to a new way of life that is founded on walking as Jesus walked. It is only when we walk as he walked that we can say that we know Jesus. It is only when we walk as he walked that we can "abide" in him. This walk is based, above all else, on love, a love exemplified in Jesus. The very love of the divine is shown through human obedience. John can obviously hold together what so many after him have tried to pull apart: belief and action, divine grace and human obedience, salvation and assurance based on practical deeds rather than abstract faith.

John stood in the tradition of scriptural writers who always knew that it was what you did that mattered. YHWH's people were called for a purpose. God moved in revelation and redemption not so that individuals could have private spiritual experiences but so that God's good, loving reign over all of creation could be brought towards fulfillment. The hope was never to escape to heaven (however conceived) when you died. The hope was that God would become King, that YHWH would dwell with his people, and that God's judgment of justice and love would flood the earth. The Torah longed for the day when the people would obey YHWH with all their mind, heart, and soul (Deut 30). The Psalms echo with the yearning for God's reign. The prophets have transformational encounters with YHWH and furiously denounce not only the idolatrous nations surrounding Israel but those within the community of faith who thought that possession of Torah or performance of cultic ritual in the absence of justice could save them. They attacked the comfortable assumptions of those who thought that because they believed the right things about God they were under no obligation to live an obedient life.

A prophet who saw through the deceit and idolatry of empty rituals and glimpsed God's heart would have agreed with John. What matters is to do justice, to love kindness, and to walk humbly with God.

———

Addicts come in as many varieties as there are people. Addiction knows no barriers of social class, wealth, education, family background, vocation, or personality. There are a complex set of factors that lead people into addiction and an equally complex set of factors that lead them out again.

Most, if not all, of the addicts I have spent time with over the years profess a desire to change. I have tended to see people at some of their lowest points, when addiction has stripped them of everything of value in their lives and is in the process of stripping them of life itself. People in such situations know what is happening; it has probably been obvious for some time that things are going wrong. In response to this knowledge addicts will profess a desire to change, whether because they actually want to or because they feel that such a profession is required of them.

Ian is caught up in his own rage and pain. The memories of years of substance abuse and the consequent breakdown of relationships are nursed close to his breast. The deaths of his children haunt him, re-lived again and again. The bitterness and anger fuel themselves and he descends into cycles of resentment, abuse, and self-abuse. In the midst of all of these wounds and all this chaos Ian always professes a desire to change. He believes that he needs to change. He believes that he will change. He believes that change is necessary, that he needs to stop drinking and get clean and find freedom.

Gerard is also an alcoholic. When I first met him his marriage had broken down, he'd lost his job, and he was homeless. The drink was stripping him of the last dregs of physical and mental health that he possessed. He was helpless in the face of a lifetime of drinking. He couldn't stop. Gerard, too, believes that he has to stop. He believes that he needs to change. He believes that change is necessary.

Ian has been in contact with many services. He has spent years talking to addiction specialists, years on prescribed medication to handle his mental health, years of access to resources beyond the imagination of addicts across the Majority World. Each time another place in a rehab comes up Ian professes again his desire and intention to change, his firm belief that he must change. And then he leaves after a few days, always with an excuse, and returns back to the addiction that may be horrible but is all that he has come to know.

Gerard went off to rehab too. He stayed the course and returned home and then relapsed back into drinking. He, too, remained firm in his belief that he needed to change. He stuck with the support groups. He got involved in various other activities. He continued to meet a counselor. Slowly, over the course of years, Gerard began to have longer and longer periods of sobriety. He discovered a freedom from alcohol that he never dreamed possible and that taste of freedom made him wanting more. Even though there are ups and down he continues to pursue freedom and make progress.

Ian's story about wanting to change starts to wear thin as the months turn to years and he refuses to do even the smallest thing that may lead to change. Gerard, on the other hand, finds himself drinking less and less and eventually becomes sober. They are both alcoholics. They started out looking and acting the same. They both said the same things throughout. The only difference was in what they *did*. One of them did want to change, and one of them did not.

Some years ago, following a baptism service where I had helped baptize a young man with whom I had had some involvement in terms of faith, a member of the congregation turned to me and said, "It must feel good, another one in the bag." The assumption was that I, and the church, could now breathe a sigh of relief. Here's another one who believes! Another one saved! We could turn our efforts to the next person who didn't yet believe "the gospel." And we wonder why we have a crisis of discipleship?

How did we get from John's passionate plea to walk as Jesus walked to this? That question is far beyond our scope here. Suffice to say that the grand Enlightenment project and the modernism to which it gave birth have cast a long shadow. Even those of us living in a post-modern world have inherited a set of abstract concepts from modernism that continue to shape our thinking, faith, and lives. Within this scheme things like "faith", "belief", and "religion" are squirreled away from, say, "politics", "economics", and "social and civic life." The former set are abstract ideas, private pursuits that may take one person one way, one another. They have very little bearing on the realities of daily life. Western Christianity, for the most part ceding the battle to this reduced and compartmentalized worldview, has only exacerbated the problem. The focus for so much "evangelism" and "mission" has been about getting people to verbally and mentally assent to some abstract statements about God, Jesus, and sin. The purpose of this, implicit or explicit, is for people to be sure that they will go to heaven when they die. This is a relentlessly individualistic ("my salvation, my relationship with God") and anti-creational ("the world's going to burn so why care about it, we'll be in heaven anyway") philosophy. The world of the real, the mundane daily world, the sin-sick, groaning world, can be left behind. It is of no ultimate importance, and therefore it is discarded. Actions are devalued and downgraded, at their very best seen as mere examples or proofs of the abstract belief that is deemed to have salvific importance. They are not less than this, but they are also much, much more. This is the point where the modernism of the Enlightenment and its heirs allies with the ever-fashionable Platonism (the ideal world is non-material) and Gnosticism (discover the divine knowledge within that will enable you to escape this evil, material world) that have for millennia denigrated this dirty, broken, and confusing creation. Abstract thought and belief are far more spiritual, far more real, than the mess we live with in our daily lives. What is Christianity about? It's about believing the right things about Jesus so that your sins are forgiven and you can, at some point, escape and go to heaven and live in bliss forever. This is a long, long way from "walking as he walked."

It is crucial for us to grasp the importance of the different conceptions of faith on offer in John and in much Western Christian thought. There is a radical difference between the two. We must remember that the word "radical" does not mean "crazy" or "mad" but rather "deep-rooted." Something that is radical goes right down to the root of things and affects everything else. That is why we start here, with the radical roots of a conception of life and faith and theology that will flower into every other area that we consider. Standing against the worldview of modernism (and the worldviews of much paganism ancient and modern) is the worldview of the people of God throughout scripture. We are not compartmentalized beings, with lives split into neat categories that we can then dissect without reference to all the others. Neither is there a hierarchy of concepts, as if abstract faith is somehow more important and therefore takes precedence over all else. We are whole persons and all our different parts interact with one another. When the people of God acted they were acting in faith. Their spirituality was political, economic, and social. Their view of God and his good creation was historical, bound up with the belief that this God had an unbreakable commitment to his creation and that he would one day put all things right. They had a history, a story, and it was going somewhere, bound up in God's story and his purposes for creation. This worldview differs in almost all respects from a common Western Christian one that focuses on individual salvation, the private pursuit of faith, and the ultimate escape from creation into non-material heaven.

Faith as currently used and understood has become an abstract idol, a shibboleth without meaning. The God we encounter in scripture and Jesus invites us into obedience, into a way of life, a way of living and knowing and being that affects everything else and changes everything. When God heard the cries of his people enslaved in Egypt he didn't say, "Just believe in me and soon you'll go to heaven where it'll all be better," but, "I have come down to deliver them from the Egyptians, and to bring them up out of that land to a good and broad land." (Exod 3:8). Indeed, the Exodus itself is the classic and paradigmatic act of the God who liberates, thereby revealing his "name" in history and speaking of the very identity and character of God. This is a theme to which we will return. When the prophets uttered their anguished pleas to a callous people they didn't urge right beliefs, right concepts about who God was, but the concrete actions of justice and peace (Isa 58; Amos 5; Mic 6). Jesus didn't invite his disciples to believe in him and go through life as usual, but to "Follow me." (Mark 1:17). James wrote his famous, "Faith without works is dead." (Jas 2:26). John, as we saw, urged the church to walk as Jesus walked. Even Paul, often hauled up as a witness for the primacy of abstract faith, at the start of his greatest letter speaks of the "obedience of faith" (Rom 1:5) and goes on to urge transformation (Rom 12:1–2) resulting in practical deeds of love and mutual welcome (Rom 12–14) that will lead to unified and multi-ethnic worship of the one true God (Rom 15). In Ephesians, following a statement about faith being a gift of God rooted in divine grace, he mentions the "good works . . . to be our way of life." (Eph 2:10). The entire scriptural canon is relentlessly focused on this creation, on praxis, on concrete actions, on real life. As Jon Sobrino, a priest living for more than fifty years among the poor of El Salvador, says, "The mere verbal proclamation of God without action to achieve his reign is not enough, and orthopraxis must take precedence over orthodoxy."[1]

Orthopraxis (right living/acting) takes priority over orthodoxy (right belief) not just because God is totally committed to his good creation, not only because it indicates and embodies orthodoxy, but because it *defines* orthodoxy. Faith actually has no existence separate from deeds; statements of belief have no meaning divorced from real life. Although the very split between abstract faith and action is in many ways an unhelpful product of modernism the primacy rests on the *following* of Jesus, on walking as he

1. Sobrino, *Christology*, 45.

walked. The disciples leaving their fishing nets behind would have had plenty of beliefs about God, about what he was doing, what he had promised, and what they hoped he would do. Perhaps they had a fascination with this strange man talking about, and increasingly acting out, the ached-for kingdom. But they would have had no clue what was in store for them, or how radically Jesus would re-shape their lives and beliefs. Their beliefs were wrong, or at least mistaken. The only way to change them, for the disciples and for us all, was to follow Jesus, to act as he acted, to walk as he walked. In that process they found orthopraxis redefining their orthodoxy. In a virtuous circle praxis and belief fed into each other, sustaining, clarifying, and deepening one another. Right living both defines and is sustained by right belief. But they started with obedience.

This would seem so obvious, both from the scriptural canon and from any serious reflection on the nature of faith, that you would think it would be accepted. Indeed, I may be thought to be guilty of caricaturing mainstream Western Christian thought by representing it as defined by the idol of abstract faith rather than obedience. Of course we act out our faith, I hear the church cry! Of course it matters what we do! This only exemplifies that the point has not been heard. The point is not that abstract faith doesn't lead to any sort of good action, of course it does. The point is that this way of thinking and living is not scriptural. It is also duplicitous, for when pushed this position will yield its ultimate answer: what matters most is what you believe. I contend that this concept is found nowhere in scripture. The difference—and it is a vast difference—is one of *importance* and *priority*. In scripture praxis, what you actually *do*, is of the ultimate importance and of first priority. Paul, early in his great epistle, talks about judgment through deeds (Rom 2); he goes on to write about accountability to God (14:10–12). Elsewhere he talks about the judgment seat of Christ to receive recompense for what has been done in the body (2 Cor 5:10). Abstract belief, as important as that is and as umbilically connected to praxis as it is, is secondary and subsidiary. Western churches, passionate about spreading the gospel, give the lie to where their priority falls: we need to get people to believe abstract creeds first, then worry about messy praxis later (if at all). This is most obviously seen in the sentimental generalizations of what passes for discipleship, where the costly and radical following of Jesus is turned into a moralizing set of precepts that can be adapted to any and every context. It doesn't really matter what you do or how you live, as long as you're basically truthful, gentle, honest, give some money away, and are generally . . . nice. What you do with the rest of your money, or your job, or your home, or your possessions, or your leisure time . . . well, that's your business.

Unfortunately you just have to mention the idea (!) of the priority of a life lived to be met with howls of derision and suspicion, particularly from Protestant quarters and particularly from those terrified of the prospect of even hinting that we could "earn our salvation" by living a morally upright life. The hoary old faith versus works debate belongs far more to the concepts and controversies of sixteenth-century Europe than to scripture and Jesus. We are whole people, created as wholes, and we cannot and must not carve out false antitheses between abstract faith and life, between body and soul, between a non-material heaven and a material earth. Scripture knows nothing of these and instead opens us up to vistas more radical, more real, and more stunning than these stunted alternatives. The one who spoke of a city set on a hill and two men building houses was concerned with real life and real actions, not abstract belief or special prayers. Jesus knew that orthopraxis mattered because it defined orthodoxy, embodying and incarnating it. The converse is also true: how you live gives the lie to what you believe. Where your treasure is, that's where we find your heart.

One of the many dangers of worshiping at the idol of abstract faith is the delusion that it creates. Consider a handful of people: a Christian, a Buddhist, a Muslim, an agnostic, a humanist, and an atheist. For the most part, in Western society, these people look pretty much the same. They have similar jobs, similar patterns of consumption, similar life-trajectories, and aspirations. In fact, modern society really needs them to look the same, to get the society or state to share values, to integrate, to work together. The only differences we might note are some private pursuits: the Christian goes to services and mid-week groups, as does the Muslim; the Buddhist meditates; the agnostic enjoys museums and the humanist is passionate about football. Private pursuits and private clubs. From all their different viewpoints they believe very different things, of course, and can articulate their various abstract positions on where we came from, if there's a god (or gods), and where we're going. From the modernist faith perspective they're very different. From the scriptural perspective they're all the same. Their abstract beliefs are at best benign thought-experiments and at worst damaging delusions. From a scriptural perspective they actually believe something very similar: the importance of earning money, of owning property, of consuming, of employment or education or economic growth, of family. From a scriptural perspective they are homogeneous. None of these things may be wrong in and of themselves. There's nothing wrong with shared values and integration and looking after your family. What does matter is priority. Treasure. Praxis. Life. These hypothetical—grossly caricatured and generalized—individuals believe, and serve, what scripture would call idols, despite their varied statements of abstract belief. Again, the powers we tend to serve is a theme to which we will return. The important point to note here is that what we might call the theology of a worldview is defined and embodied by the praxis of those concerned. What you do shows what, or whom, you believe most, what you give priority to. Is a Christian a Christian who not only stops his ears to the cries of the poor of the world but continues to live in ways that keep those oppressive structures in place? "Lord, Lord, we cast out demons in your name." And Jesus says, "I never knew you." (Matt 7:22–23).

The language and priority of orthopraxis, of walking as Jesus walked, also subverts and sidesteps another modernist folly: the myth of objectivity. If we relegate faith to the abstract sphere where we can discuss it, question it, study it, propagate it, and preach it without too much reference to deeds then we can succumb to the delusion that we can appropriate faith from a supposed neutral ground. This is in fact where most people live and choose their "spiritual" options: a bit of all the things that seem good, whose ideas appeal to me, that attract me. I am a neutral observer, picking what I choose, like a supermarket shopper poring over the vegetable aisle. Or rather, I'm a discerning customer dawdling through the market, with various stalls setting out their abstract wares, sometimes in competition with one another, and inviting me to come and "believe." This is folly. Every choice we make, and the ones that we don't make consciously, incarnates a particular set of beliefs, a theology. Society itself holds and embodies a particular theology, a particular way of telling stories about the world and meaning and purpose and importance, that we live within whether we like it or not. This is as true for those worldviews that acknowledge a deity (or more) as for those that do not. We are constantly embodying what we believe, whether we give thought to it or not and whether we acknowledge it or not. It is telling that there is so much dissonance between what people *say* they believe, and may well *think* they believe, and what is actually defined as their belief through their *praxis*. This is inescapable. There is no careful, safe place from which to disinterestedly observe the options open for us. Faith, properly understood, is a continuous choice of action rather than an abstract belief. It is a choice shown most truly in what we do rather than what we say we believe. "Those who say, 'I love God', and hate their brothers and sisters, are liars." (1 John 4:20). "Show me your faith without works, and I by my works will show you my faith." (Jas 2:18b). It is the way that you walk that tells the world what you believe, not some set of verbally or mentally assented-to statements. It's the way you live that defines the faith you hold.

When we shift the debate to the way we live and what we do we escape the sordid and sterile abstractions that have sullied so much Christian theology and mission. Instead of circular abstract debates trying to prove or disprove various bits of dogma or scriptural interpretation we find that the "proof" of any such creed or perspective is in the lives then lived, not the supposed coherence of an abstract argument. Instead of a fanatical insistence on praying a certain prayer, assenting to a certain belief, or making some one-off decision we find that Christian life is defined by walking in a certain way, by certain specific ways of life. On wider horizons we find that Christian engagement with the world is marked by praxis rather than abstract belief. Inter-faith discussion and disagreement rests now on lives lived—the fruit produced—rather than abstract beliefs or conceptions about God, the divine, ultimate meaning, and purpose. The strained relationship between faith and science, with some desperate to drive a wedge between them and others desperate to use one to prove the other, is radically relativized because what matters is how you live and not the theories you hold. The terms of the debate are firmly couched in the life you live and the deeds you do. There are doubtless many objections to this position but the point is that the proof of this or any alternative scheme is found not in arguments on a page but in the lives (and world) produced. It is the fruit that matters. Much of the troubled reflections in these pages have stemmed from the realization that communities supposedly confessing all the right abstract beliefs have yet produced awful, bitter fruit. Something is wrong, or at the very least misplaced.

If we have sidestepped the myth of objectivity, seeing it as a hopeless and arrogant idol, then it is important to note that we also sidestep subjectivity. The post-modernist, happy to collapse everything back to the self (itself then deconstructed) is as deluded as the modernist thinking that he has found the objective, disinterested ground. The Christian gloss on subjectivism is that attitude that reduces all matters of faith and life to "my relationship with God." As long as my heart is right before God then nothing else matters. I make my moral choices in splendid isolation and private communion with my deity and it is for no one else to judge them or dare to call them into question. After all, I *feel* that it's right. To the unscriptural backwaters and idolatrous follies of objectivity and subjectivity orthopraxis demands a focus on and priority of the life lived. Even those most committed to subjectivity eat, drink, and do something with their days, and therefore embody a faith-in-praxis that we can observe.

There is a certain non-negotiable factor to praxis. You can approve or disapprove of my praxis (and therefore the faith it embodies) but you cannot deny what I do. You cannot deny the praxis itself. This is most true when we consider love, particularly the love of God in Jesus. The entire scriptural canon bears witness to the God who acts in love, a God so committed to his creation that he will personally bear the hostility and pain of the sin-sick world to reconcile it to himself. In the life, death, and resurrection of Jesus we have the supreme example of orthopraxis, the God who doesn't ask us to believe in an abstract truth but shows us what love truly looks like in the life that is most fully life. Perhaps this public aspect of orthopraxis is what Paul meant when he wrote that, "It was before your eyes that Jesus Christ was publicly exhibited as crucified!" (Gal 3:1). That is, in the life of the apostle the Galatians had seen the unmistakable marks of the new creation inaugurated by and in Jesus. Paul's praxis showed them what it meant to follow a crucified Messiah as their King.

There is no better argument or critique of the status quo than orthopraxis. Instead of exhausting ourselves in an endless attempt to get people to believe certain things we are freed to focus on the good, on the kingdom, and allow our lives to shine in the midst of a crooked and perverse generation (Phil 2:15). If we want to persuade people that Jesus is the way, the truth, and the life then we must be people embodying truth and life as we walk that way. This leads to a model of engagement and critique that is relentlessly focused on the good. I do not need to argue with you, to try and persuade you with abstract arguments or knowledge; I need to act justly, to love kindness, and to walk humbly with God (Mic 6:8) towards his kingdom. This is the cast-iron credibility of praxis. If we are correct and this way in and of Jesus does indeed lead to truth and life then this will be obvious to all. Of course, scripture is under no illusion that this will mean widespread acceptance of the gospel, quite the opposite in fact. It will more often mean hostility and aggression from those who stand condemned not because they believe something different but because they are threatened by the truly human lives of the redeemed people. Though the nations malign us, they won't be able to deny our good deeds (1 Pet 2:12). The ambivalence of the response to the gospel—the proclamation and embodying of Jesus as king—is exemplified in Acts 5:13, where people are both attracted and terrified by the church. There is something joyous and something threatening about a way of life that promises to be in the process of setting all things to right at last. At a stroke we see the desperate need for a fresh emphasis on praxis, on lifestyle, on deeds, as *the* defining element of Christian mission and discipleship. We have huddled for too long in small groups studying scripture and increasing our abstract belief and knowledge. The call for simple but demanding—indeed, cruciform—obedience has gone unheard for too long.

Orthopraxis is the only thing that gives credibility but it is also the only thing that gives authority. There is a paradoxical power in the humiliated praxis of the cross. The powers and those formed by them may rage against it but they, even they, will find that love never fails. The sole source of all our credibility and authority lies in what we do. Not what we believe. Not what we say. Not the social or civic positions that we occupy. What we do. The way we walk. Authority and credibility are earned through the hard, mundane faithfulness of service. This is what Jesus points to, not only in his life but also in his words about true leaders becoming slaves (Luke 22:24–27). Slavery is what Jesus took upon himself (Phil 2:7) and we are invited to share in and imitate our King (Phil 2:5). In a world where almost all conceptions of authority carry with them the threat of violence and coercive power the orthopraxis of slavery and the cross stand in marked contrast. This should not surprise us, for we all know that those who have the power to move us most in life are those whom we love and who love us. Fear and violence, although universally used to enforce social conformity, find that they cannot in the end have power over us. Only those who love and live in love can speak into broken lives and a broken world the word that restores to fullness of life. Here again we see Jesus as the one who can command obedience only because he is our slave, because he loved so fully. Paradoxical power and undeniable credibility and authority.

The first-century world was just as awash with competing ideologies, powers, theologies, and answers to life's questions as the twenty-first century one. Jesus and the early church knew that the only thing that could hold you steady to the kingdom of God was praxis. When you're wondering who is true and who is false, and people are saying they believe all sorts of things, where do you turn to find proof? You look at the fruit of their lives. You look at what they do. Jesus, Peter, James, John, Paul, they all insist on praxis, on deeds done, as the determining factor marking out those in the kingdom and those outside (and, more importantly, those who claim they're in but in fact are not). There's no point quizzing people over an abstract list of beliefs that anyone could reel off. Look at what they do. Out of the overflow of the heart the mouth speaks, and the life is lived. Abstract belief is always in service to praxis.

Before we turn everything over to praxis, however, we sound a note of caution. The danger with praxis, and one of the reasons why we resist conceptualizing faith in these terms, is that we are ragged, halfhearted, contradictory creatures. How can we walk as Jesus walked? We cannot, and if we cannot we stand self-condemned. We are not perfect disciples. We are all painfully aware of the horrors and shortcomings of the church, the one who looks a lot less like a pure and beautiful bride and a lot more like a deceiving, damaged, and damaging whore. Is this our God? This is the tension that has driven faith into the desert of abstraction. We are terrified of our own brokenness, and what that might say about our God. In technical terms this is the danger of an over-realized eschatology, of equating what we do now with the fullness of God and his kingdom. We fear the mocking of hypocrisy that will stain our God. Here we need the tension of the now and not yet kingdom. Rather than trying to escape again to an unsullied abstraction where, thankfully, we don't have to worry too much about the awful mess we're in (after all, our sins are forgiven, our hearts are right before God, and it'll be nice in heaven when we die) we must instead take the route of obedience, and follow. Praxis, humble and humiliated and broken though it may be, is still all we have. The disciples got up and followed Jesus without knowing or believing anything "right", and Jesus invited them to walk as he walked. If Jesus is the way then he's the way to something or someone, and although we may be on the path we're not there yet. It isn't all right. The kingdom is here, but not fully. We need to learn to live in this tension, as hard as that is and as painful as that is, and to insist that both how we live defines what we believe *and* that Jesus is always calling us to something better. We are not yet converted. The fulfillment of the kingdom is always over our horizons. We can never reduce the kingdom of God, or God himself, to our fractured praxis, just as we cannot glimpse God or enter the kingdom without praxis.

At the heart of our refusal to consider orthopraxis—embodied theology—as having prime importance is just how dangerous and messy and radical it is. Praxis is about all our life, not just the abstract beliefs we hold. Up for debate then are all those things we shy away from in the church and in society, all those things we hold so private and so precious: what you spend your money on, your leisure time, your job, your home, your family, your pension. Orthopraxis demands a quite specific obedience in every area— to think through and act on all of life with Jesus as King—and is therefore a much more terrifying prospect than recalibrating some abstract beliefs. We have been afraid of judging others, of rank hypocrisy, but this is only because we fail to grasp the essential goodness of praxis. To walk after Jesus is not to condemn those who do not, or who are not so far along the way, but to offer a living example of faith, hope, and love. This is no judgment but a joyous encouragement towards the good. The kingdom is not our own, nor is our path a lonely, individualistic one concerned with my personal salvation and purity. It is by definition a communal enterprise. A body. We need to provoke one another to love and good deeds (Heb 10:24). Community, walking together, is the essence of love. Praxis is radical, dangerous, and world-changing. There will be crosses to be borne, deaths to suffer, the relinquishment of things held on to for so long, but there is the joy and the hope and the promise of a good kingdom and a good King. There is a murmur of a way of love that brings us into truth and life. If we start to walk this way we will find that it is no sacrifice to lose our abstractions and gain our very being.

If we are people of the way, then, people marked and known by praxis, can we then disregard all that abstract belief as so much unnecessary baggage? By no means! If faith without works is dead then works without faith are deaf, blind, and dumb. It is simply a matter of priority. Abstract belief is in service of the life lived. Always. Our praxis then feeds back to question, sustain, and inform abstract belief, and vice versa, but praxis is always prior. We follow Jesus, then we know him, then we can believe. That was the route the disciples took and that must be our route too. Abstract debate, ideas, creeds, dogmas, doctrine, beliefs, all of these are important but only insofar as they are defined and embodied in praxis. It matters what we do. That's all that matters. A Christian theology is always an embodied theology of doing, of praxis. Of course, we can argue that the only reason we do what we do is because of what we believe, or that we can only do what we do because of what we believe, but even here it is the *doing* that matters. To return to Ian and Gerard, what matters is what we do. Not what we say or the statements that we make but what actually happens, even if the road to freedom is marked by many cycles of failure and stumbling. The church needs her abstract thinkers, needs her scholars and studies and academia, needs her abstract debate and definition. The church needs these things more than ever in a culture that denigrates the role of intellectual effort and striving. These gifts to the body, however, always serve within a context, and that context must be the sustaining, clarifying, and enabling of orthopraxis. Without this they become ends in themselves, self-absorbed and idolatrous. As if one could ever discuss theories of justice or peace without actually seeking to embody them! Or worse, while living a lifestyle that demands injustice and conflict to sustain it! Yet such is the absurdity of so much Western Christian discourse, in hock to an idol of abstraction that leaves us incapable of walking in the path of obedience.

Here our modernist language and concepts—of the abstract and the concrete, the subjective and the objective—break down and become unhelpful. John writes of love, and love is something that has to involve others. Love is never objective or subjective, neither staying aloof nor collapsing back into itself, but it is self-involving. We cannot properly understand love unless we live it; it is participatory by nature. So is orthopraxis. So is theology. Love *is* orthopraxis, for love cannot but express itself in practical deeds seeking the good of another. We love because he first loved us. We walk as Jesus walked not because we are caught up in a ceaseless striving for an unattainable perfection but because we abide in him. We stand by the life lived, yet find that this life is not just our life but the life of the Messiah who lives in me, who loves me and gave himself for me. It is not just our life, but our life caught up with the community of all those who are bound together into one body, the Messiah's body, the Messiah's life. We are brought by love into the very life of God and this is the radical change that urged these men and women of faith to lay down their whole selves for one another and for God.[2] This is knowing through and by love, an epistemology of love. This is abiding and participating in love, an ontology of love. This is walking and living in love, a praxis of love. And where do we see love? How do we know what it is? How dare we begin to walk or believe? There is a man who says, "Follow", who says, "Come, you who are weary", who forgives as he's nailed to a cross. There's a King and a kingdom that look different from anything we've ever known. And there's a tomb that stands empty and breathes of a new creation where everything is going to be set right . . .

———————

Graih is a small charity seeking to serve the homeless on the Isle of Man. I have been involved with it for many years. It grew from the smallest of roots: the faithfulness of a few individuals opening a

---

2. See Fiddes, *Participating in God.* This is arguably an example of orthodoxy in service to orthopraxis, as Fiddes seeks to develop a "pastoral doctrine of the Trinity" focused on communion with the life and love of God.

drop-in for men who were alcoholic. As relationships were formed it became obvious to the volunteers that the guys coming in were not only alcoholic but often sleeping rough in public toilets and squats. With fear and trembling and the blessing of the church the drop-in opened for a few months over winter overnight to give shelter to those who were homeless. There weren't even any beds, just ancient sofas, but it was better than being outside. Unbeknownst to the volunteers running the drop-in (who still had little idea that a charity would ever be formed from their work) there was a high-level multi-agency group comprising top civil servants, heads of charities, and faith leaders meeting to discuss the "issue" of homelessness. In those early seasons gradual connections were formed and the volunteers of the drop-in were eventually invited into the meetings. It was obvious that these were two groups from different worlds. There were those who knew men who were homeless and spent their nights dozing on sofas next to them, and there were those who spoke of strategies and policies and procedures. The volunteers, untrained and unprofessional, knew that what mattered was serving those in need. The multi-agency group, shaped by a statutory mentality, knew that what mattered was formulating the right policies. The multi-agency group decided that a charity was needed, a charity that would serve as an umbrella organization for a wide array of "homelessness issues", including the drop-in. Documents were drawn up, funding put in place, staff appointed, and procedures drafted. It was then apparent that there was a problem. This new charity actually had little or no contact with homeless people. They had everything in place, all the abstract boxes ticked, but they had no praxis.

The government approached the volunteers at the drop-in (which had by this point coalesced into its own charity, Graih) and asked them to take over some government premises to run as a shelter. The language of partnership was used. When the volunteers inquired as to whether the homeless guys could paint the walls or make a cup of tea they were told that such activities could only be undertaken by government-appointed contractors and those with food safety and hygiene certificates. And risk assessments would have to be done on everybody. The volunteers pointed out that they intentionally took risks to build relationships with risky people and that allowing the guys ownership of small tasks was a really big part of their successful praxis. They were ignored. Those well-versed in procedural abstractions could not believe or trust a praxis-driven group of amateurs. Although partnership was spoken of it was clear where the power would lie: in the abstract formulations of legal necessities and policies rather than actual praxis and real people. The volunteers decided not to take up the offer. A shelter was opened anyway, complete with risk assessments and procedures. It closed after a few months due to lack of use.

You may think that one group who has no relationship with people who are homeless might choose to listen to another group that spends a lot of time with those who are homeless. You may think it would be obvious where credibility and authority lie. Yet the powerful appeal of abstract meetings, words, positions, procedures, policies, strategies, and risk assessments tend to exclude those who choose a different approach. Who walk a different way. Divorced from praxis, this bloated abstract edifice collapsed. If you start with what you believe, what you think, the abstract ruminations and principles, but never *do* anything, you have nothing. If you start with action and let that inform your abstract formulations you may not stray too far. All your abstractions must always be in the service of praxis; they exist only insofar as they liberate, clarify, deepen, and sustain praxis. It doesn't matter what you believe. What matters is what you do.

Chapter 2

The God of Liberation and the Idol of Freedom

God also spoke to Moses . . . 'I am the LORD. I appeared to Abraham, Isaac, and Jacob as God Almighty, but by my name "The LORD" I did not make myself known to them. I also established my covenant with them . . . I have also heard the groaning of the Israelites, whom the Egyptians are holding as slaves, and I have remembered my covenant. Say therefore to the Israelites, "I am the LORD, and I will free you from the burdens of the Egyptians and deliver you from slavery to them. I will redeem you with an outstretched arm and with mighty acts of judgement. I will take you as my people, and I will be your God. You shall know that I am the LORD your God, who has freed you from the burdens of the Egyptians . . . " Moses told this to the Israelites, but they would not listen to Moses, because of their broken spirit and their cruel slavery.

—Exodus 6:2–9

But when the fullness of time had come, God sent his Son, born of a woman, born under the law, in order to redeem those who were under the law, so that we might receive adoption as children. And because you are children, God has sent the Spirit

of his Son into our hearts, crying, 'Abba! Father!' So you are
no longer a slave but a child, and if a child then also an heir,
through God. Formerly, when you did not know God, you were
enslaved to beings that by nature are not gods. Now, however,
that you have come to know God, or rather to be known by
God, how can you turn back again to the weak and beggarly
elemental spirits?

—GALATIANS 4:4–9

GOD IS THE GOD who liberates. When God went down to Egypt
and heard the cries of his people it wasn't just that he rescued them
but that in this rescue his name was revealed. Through the act of
liberation we see who God is. Liberation is revelation. Along with
the call of Abram in Genesis 12 the Exodus became the foundation
of Israel's understanding of who God was, is, and what he would
do. God heard them in their slavery and God acted. He brought
them out to be a priestly kingdom and a holy nation (Exod 19:6),
he gave them the Torah in the theophany at Sinai. His glory dwelt
amongst them (Exod 40:34–38). When the people of God longed
for him to act again in redemption they looked back to the Exodus
(Neh 9:9–15; Dan 9:15), for through it God had "made himself a
name." When Israel's story was told and re-told the Exodus fea-
tured prominently (Pss 77, 78, 80, 81, 105, 106, 114, 136), often
with the longing that God would again act in deliverance. The
prophets were full of memories of the God of the Exodus and they
pointed forward to an even greater Exodus, a deliverance that
would not only restore and redeem God's people but would flow
out to all nations and all creation (Isa 40–66; Jer 31; Ezek 36–37).
This was the hope of Israel, the renewal of the covenant, the end of
exile and slavery, the restoration of how things should be. When
we come to the NT we should not be surprised to find a prophet
enacting the Red Sea crossing in the baptisms in the Jordan, or
thousands of people being fed in the wilderness, or a wonderful
teaching being given from a mountainside. Something immense
was happening. God was moving, acting, liberating. The kingdom

was coming. And Paul, writing to the fledgling churches, is soaked in the language of slavery and freedom, of passing through the waters into a new life and God's dwelling in us by the Spirit, of the new Exodus that fully reveals who God is (Rom 6, 8; Gal 4).

Exodus imagery and theology undergirds and enlivens many aspects of scripture but the central point for our current purposes is this: the liberation that reveals God, the Exodus, is not primarily individual and not primarily what we might call "spiritual." To be sure, individual Israelites were saved, but they were part of something much, much bigger. Our slippery term "spiritual" certainly covers some aspects of Exodus liberation but for the slaves of Egypt the redemption was social, political, and economic (all of which, incidentally, are very much "spiritual" matters in scripture, much to the chagrin of modern thought), covering all aspects of life. Every facet of Israel's life was redeemed, and they were redeemed for a specific purpose: not heading off to heaven to be with God forever but to be a "blessing to the nations." (Gen 12:1–3; Deut 4; Isa 49).

———◦———

I have sat with Bobby many times. Often we have sat in his flat, surrounded by the detritus of his life, struggling to pull together some hope. Bobby was unwanted from a young age. His childhood was full of difficulties. His early adult years were marked by attempts at work and a slow, painful deterioration of his mental health, fueled by alcohol, fear, and a whole host of bad acquaintances. He ended up on the streets. Now he's clawed his way back to a flat, desperate to cobble together some pretense of normality. His flat is a representation of his mind and soul: full of rubbish, unwashed clothes and dishes, piles of useless tat gleaned from all over the place. Simply to sit there and stare at the tangled mess spilling over in every room is to feel the weight of despair, like a black hole, drag you down into apathy. It all just seems too much. Where do you begin to even start to clear up? It's a mass, physical and mental (and spiritual), that drags him down. He's been on anti-depressants for years. His doctor keeps on doling out the pills, tacitly acknowledging that there's little else to be done save to keep on swallowing the meds and existing. He is still, in so many ways, a terrified child, trying to make his way in an adult world that repeatedly rejects him. He has no purpose, few skills, and no hope.

Bobby has also been around the church for a while. He's been baptized, prayed the prayers, attended meetings, even made some tentative friendships in the congregation. He struggles to read his bible (his literacy isn't great) and often gets overwhelmed by feelings of guilt, knowing that he's not a good Christian and yet at the same time unable to summon up the motivation or desire to do those good Christian things like daily devotionals and private prayer. Bobby remains scared and alone, so immature and fearful that he's incapable of making good decisions. There is a broken spirit and a cruel slavery that robs him of the capacity to imagine life differently, the capacity to hope.

———◦◦———

I've lost count of the number of times I've been in prayer meetings and things have kicked off with a "thank you God that we have the freedom to worship . . . " I know what people are trying to say. They are grateful that we can gather without harassment to pray, read the bible, and sing some songs. There's nothing wrong with that. It's just that none of these things have much to do with the scriptural concepts of freedom and worship. To continue to think of freedom and worship in terms of being safe enough to gather and sing some songs is to do a grave disservice to both freedom and worship and to delude ourselves that we're enjoying both when actually we have neither.

Now, I have lived my entire life in one of the safest, quietest, most affluent places there has ever been. I am grateful for these things. I am well aware that many of my family around the globe cannot meet to pray or study scripture or sing songs. Many are harassed, discriminated against, and killed. I am not denigrating the tolerance I enjoy, and neither minimizing nor glorifying the seriousness of their sufferings and their plight. There is much that we, in cloistered confines of the safe Western church, have to learn from brothers and sisters in harsher environments; just as there is much more that we should do to help those suffering. Yet these cloistered confines are the context I live and breathe, and the triumphs we think we enjoy may well turn out to be something more insidious than we imagined.

Liberation is the gift of God. "Where the Spirit of the Lord is, there is freedom." (2 Cor 3:17). Our freedom is dependent on God alone, not the state's attitude towards us or the surrounding cultural climate. This is because the liberation that God brings is deeper and richer than the instant sociopolitical context, although not divorced from it. We live and move have our being in someone other than the many gods and many idols of the world around us, and it is to the same degree that we choose to follow Jesus no matter where we find ourselves that we find our deepest liberation and our true humanity. The state does not give freedom. The will of the people does not grant liberation. We were bought at a price, and this gift is the gift of God (1 Cor 6:20). The NT is clear, in fact, that the very concept of freedom might be a tricky one. We all serve somebody, or something. Jesus talks of heart and treasure, of being unable to serve two masters, of a yoke that is nevertheless easy and light (Matt 6:19–21, 24; 11:28–30). The passage in John 8 is instructive for our entire theme here, not only in walking in the truth and freedom of the "light of the world" but for the role of Jesus as the sole bringer of freedom (not social position, surrounding cultural climate, or ethnicity). Paul talks about the two different kinds of "slavery" in Romans 6, while pointing out in the Galatians passage above that apart from Jesus and the Spirit people are enslaved. In Philippians 2 he urges us to imitate Jesus, who took slavery upon himself. We're all slaves, but there might just be a master who leads to liberation.

Liberation for what? If there's freedom on offer, perhaps a different sort of freedom than the world envisages, what's it for? What it manifestly isn't for, in scripture, is singing a few songs together and feeling happy that, since our sins have been forgiven, we're bound for heaven sooner or later. To call this "worship" borders on the blasphemous. (An interesting line of study would be to look at the link between persecution and worship throughout the history of the people of God. Although persecution isn't a good thing it is something that is expected throughout scripture as the hallmark of God's faithful people in confrontation with a rebellious and fractured world. Remember the strange joy of the early church to be counted "worthy to suffer dishonor for the sake of the name?" [Acts 5:41; 1 Pet 4:13]. Perhaps our supposed freedom rests on the inoffensive nature of our supposed worship. Why bother to disagree with something so harmless and nice? But time would fail us to tell of such things . . .).

Our liberation is into humanity, our created goodness and identity that from Genesis onwards was God's purpose for creation. We were put in the garden to serve it (Gen 2:15) and by so doing to bring all of creation's inarticulate praise to the creator. Kings and priests, serving God's creation in peace and justice and bringing its worship back to God (Exod 19:6; Ps 8; Rev 5:10). This is God's overarching purpose towards which liberation always points and of which the Exodus under Moses was but a small foretaste. The prophets knew this, looking to God to implement his kingdom of peace and justice so that the lion might live with the lamb (Isa 11), that creation would burst into fullness of life and praise (Isa 55), that the river of life would flood the earth with healing (Ezek 47). There's a good reason why Jesus opened the scroll of Isaiah and read words of jubilee and freedom in a synagogue at Nazareth in Luke 4 (a royal announcement of God's liberation that instantly incurred disbelief and persecution). The early Christians knew that God's kingdom had arrived in the life, death, and resurrection of Jesus. God's wonderful new creation, his setting of all things to right at last, had broken in (2 Cor 5:17). And even though the kingdom was not here fully they were to live as citizens of new creation, ambassadors of a different kingdom, of heaven (Phil 3:20–21).

As is often pointed out, the purpose of citizenship in Roman times was not so that the citizens could one day retire to Rome (in fact, part of the whole institution of citizenship was to stop this happening as Rome was far too overcrowded to accommodate everyone) but that they could bring all the benefits of Roman civilization to the cities and countries where they now dwelt. Christians at Philippi (a Roman colony) were being asked to embody the life of heaven on earth (cf. Matt 6:10). As the people of the new Exodus, the full and final liberation, even though they walked through the wilderness of a world not yet suffused with God's glory, a world groaning in hope (Rom 8), they had the Spirit with them, God in their midst, an assurance of the inheritance (Eph 1:13–14) that is no longer a small geographical patch of land but the whole world (Rom 4:13, 5:17). This is what God was always purposing, what Abraham was called for, what the liberation meant. In the resurrection God's new creation had burst into history and everything was changed. One day the Messiah would hand the kingdom over to the Father, one day God would be all in all, one day what was mortal and corruptible would be swallowed up with the incorruption and immortality of a more full, more real, more *physical*, resurrection body and death would be no more (1 Cor 15). One day the whole life of heaven would be the whole life of earth, as the garden becomes a city and the river of life heals the nations (Rev 21–22). This, in all its facets and beauty, all its grandeur and wonder, all its joy and love and justice, is liberation. True freedom. Salvation. Anything less is a sham.

It should be obvious that this scriptural hope of liberation, with its breathtaking sweep of vision that encompasses every aspect of creation and affects it radically, stands in stark contrast with the usual Western Christian story of an individual's sin, an individual's relationship with Jesus, and an individual's hope of heaven. Individuals are saved from sin, of course, and this is a joyous part of God's liberation, but it is only a *part*. There's no point huddling in awe and wonder around a seed; it has to fall to the ground, die, and be raised as part of something greater. There's no point forsaking the fountain of living water and digging out our own cisterns, cracked and incapable of holding even the feeble drips we place into them (Jer 2:13). We belong to something bigger. To reduce salvation, freedom, and worship to an individual's relationship with God and a weekly service is to act like Esau, trading our birthright for a mess of pottage (Gen 25:29–34).

The problem that Bobby had, along with many others like him, was that he wasn't free to worship. He was still in bondage under the same old slavemasters, everything from the individual fears and desires to the wider societal patterns that had systematically demeaned and rejected him. Bobby isn't free, and his broken spirit and cruel slavery means that he's almost incapable of receiving the announcement of God's liberation. When, in this state of slavery, Bobby hears Christians thanking God for their freedom to worship (and he knows at some level that he's not free, that he's struggling and failing), we have entered the realm of idolatry. For too long the church has proclaimed a spurious freedom and a spurious worship to those still in slavery, and done nothing to participate in God's kingdom, God's liberation. Don't worry that your mind, heart, body, and soul are in tatters, that you sit in the lowering darkness surrounded by rubbish, that your days are an endless re-run of shallow aimlessness, filth, and failure . . . you're saved and free to worship! You're headed for heaven! This is facile.

One of the central arguments of this book is that we are not free, and often blind to our own slavery. There's nothing as safe as the slave who thinks he's free, for the liberation that could be his will forever remain unsought. When we dress up our slavery in the fine drag of Babylon, bow down and proclaim how wonderful our "freedom" is as we "worship" then we can be sure that the idols smile to themselves. Their reign is unchallenged. I am not against gathering together without hindrance, or singing songs and listening to sermons—I enjoy all of these—but let's not confuse them with the far greater and more radical reality.

What Bobby needs is the full-orbed liberation that God has both started and yearns to complete (and of which the church is invited to be both the bearer and the embodied message of such good news). He needs to be called to participate in something greater, to be welcomed into a family, to have people to live with, eat with, work with. A salvation that focuses on an abstract "forgiveness of sins" might work very well for the affluent middle classes who live relatively stable lives and hold some sort of normality together; it manifestly does not do much for, and may even further damage, those more fractured on the margins of society.

It is noteworthy that we find ourselves in such a position after slicing the connection between "forgiveness of sins" and the concrete sociopolitical realities of the peace and justice of God's kingdom. The first century knew little of the troubled introspective conscience of modern Western Christians and a lot more of the reality that God's forgiveness of sins *meant* life in justice and peace. For too long we've seen the twin poles of God's kingdom—peace and justice—as optional extras to some other concept of salvation. They're nice things to do, of course, especially for the socially-minded of the faith, but they're not as important as "being saved." What is sometimes disparagingly called "the social gospel", or the fundamental human mandate of caring and serving creation, are not additional to salvation, they *are* salvation. I was once asked what was "Christian" about campaigning for environmental justice. When we can inhabit a faith where such fundamental concepts like environmentalism, like social justice, like relief of poverty and sickness, are not really "Christian" then we can be sure that we have strayed far from anything that scripture would recognize as salvation. My interlocutor pointed out that lots of non-Christian groups are at the forefront of such movements (Greenpeace, for example). That's hardly an argument against pursuing justice and peace on all fronts and more of a slur on a church that smugly sits back and thinks she's OK because she's headed off to heaven. The tax-collectors and prostitutes are entering the kingdom before us . . . (Matt 21:31). To this stunted and shriveled version of salvation God too proclaims liberation: the vision of justice for individuals, families, and races, for the entire created order, the vision of all of these relationships characterized by the peace of God.[1]

This holistic redemption is not so much believed as lived. It it not so much preached as embodied. We are again in the realm of costly but beautiful orthopraxis, focused on participating in the

1. For the wider horizons of mission see Wright, *Mission of God; Mission of God's People.* For an arresting analysis of the church defined by mission see Driver, *Images of the Church.*

goodness of God's kingdom rather than seeking to believe certain things about it (this might draw us into company with some interesting and unlikely bedfellows, who want to know nothing of Jesus but are passionate about justice . . . what part do they have in the kingdom?). Bobby needs to *join* something good and not just *believe* something good. Mission and discipleship are about life, not belief.

Shed of our shackles of slavery, under the yoke a very different master, we can lift up our heads and gaze in wonder and astonishment at the vistas now open before us. Without the pretense of what we currently call freedom and worship we can focus on our glorious inheritance. Throughout the coming section—a case study, if you like, of salvation—we see that the call is always to conversion. There are layers of liberation, depths to our new-found freedom, and to explore them is part of the delight and wonder of discipleship. And more, for the more we understand and live out of our freedom and true humanity the more we actually participate in the kingdom that is coming and help bring about its consummation. We are in a process of being converted, the end is God as all in all (1 Cor 15:28).

There has been much made in the last generation or so of the sacred and secular split, and how this is overcome. This is a good thing. The whole created order is God's. End of debate. I belong to a generation for whom the very concept of such a divide is an odd one. Life is a whole and faith even more so. How could it ever be otherwise? With the basic divide done away with we can look at far more important questions and there is no area that exemplifies this so well as work.

One of the great gains of the dissolution of the sacred and secular split has been the insight that our jobs are part of God's mission. They are not just "mission fields" where we might meet some unbeliever but have intrinsic worth and the capacity to participate in God's kingdom. Unfortunately the discourse has often stopped there, content with sacralising all the work of God's people and exhorting them to go off and labor for the kingdom. In the worst cases this boils down to "be a good employee" and the importance of honesty and integrity in the workplace (as if this should need to be reiterated to those following Jesus!). No one ever asks what sort of work we should do.

I know many people to whom God has given wonderful skills and who have employed them in successful drug dealing. If such a person chooses to follow Jesus what are they to do? They could deal illegal drugs in an honest, non-violent way, using their trade to meet all sorts of people who would usually stay far away from the church. What about prostitutes? It could be a great opportunity to serve and meet a whole host of varied characters. When these questions are raised among the respectable Christian middle classes they are met with derision and treated as extreme absurdities. If pressed the answer as to why such people should give up their professions as part of following Jesus is that such activities are illegal or intrinsically damaging. This is odd. On the one hand the church professes that the world dwells in darkness and needs the light of Christ (see John), while on the other hand out-sourcing moral questions and decisions to the state! The role of legality and the state will be looked at in more detail in the next chapter. The hypocrisy of this position renders it void. So too the argument about certain activities being intrinsically damaging or sinful; it's all very well as long as we're consistent. It's strange that these activities tend to get narrowed down to everyone's favorite sins: sex and drugs. The church tells the drug dealer to leave it all behind but welcomes the stockbroker who's just helped push the price of grain up and left an extra ten million people facing starvation. Out with the prostitutes, but happy to accept the tithes of the engineer working in the big arms factory selling munitions killing people around the world. Or the investment banker who gambled pension funds and brought economic ruin across the globe. Or the army of lawyers, accountants, administrators, and associated professions who make such activities possible. I have sat with Christian leaders and heard them declare how important it is that Christians work in the e-gaming industry, facilitating futile and damaging gambling across the world, because the light of Jesus needs to shine in the darkest places. As if you could only ever proclaim salvation to a prostitute by *being* a prostitute, or to a dealer by *being* an addict. There must be a better way than this.

To this mess, this madness that has gone from locking the sacred up on a Sunday to sacralising everything under the sun, the benefit of a clearer vision of God's kingdom must be brought. If we are clear about the liberation that God brings and the impact that this has over all our lives then our work is brought into proper perspective. Our work only has meaning and purpose insofar as it participates in the kingdom of God. This both broadens and narrows our concept of work. It broadens it because the kingdom affects all areas of life and human endeavor. The artist and the scholar are called to participate in the kingdom along with the lawyer and the accountant, the builder and the doctor, the musician and the craftswoman. It narrows it because God's kingdom and the liberation it brings are very specific, focused on those twin poles of peace and justice.

The lawyer championing access to the legal system for those with no money, little education, and few resources participates in the kingdom; the lawyer helping a multinational corporation like Monsanto sue Indian farmers for trying to save their seeds does not. The banker seeking to help people manage and reduce their debt and encouraging financial wisdom participates in the kingdom; the banker investing on the stock market and contributing to the volatility of basic food prices around the world does not. The accountant enabling charities to organize their finances and therefore releasing people to do the work participates; the accountant enabling the global rich, both individuals and companies, to escape paying their taxes where they earn their money through complex offshore arrangements does not. The engineer designing technology to improve the lives of disabled people participates; the engineer designing munitions to disable people does not. We could go on, and in fact it is urgent that the church should go on, enabling and encouraging the people of God to work out what their vocation means in the light of God's liberation. If we call the drug dealer and the prostitute away from a life that courts death then we must also call the investment banker, the insurance broker, and the e-gaming executive. They are all involved in selling commodities in ways that are anti-human and therefore anti-God, whether illegal drugs, sex, or complex financial instruments and gambling.

All of these miniature discussions about the viability of certain activities or professions in fact take place within a much larger world of work that is itself challenged by the news of God's liberation, subverted by the true life of the kingdom. Most of us live in an economic system of capitalism. Capitalism as we experience it depends on the sweat, blood, and tears of the vast majority of the world's population and the natural resources of their lands to create wealth that flows to the affluent minority. Capitalism depends on systemic injustice and the oppression of the poor by the rich. John saw through the same patterns in Revelation 17–18 and called it right: the whore of Babylon. It is not, as once described to me, "the worst economic system apart from all the rest" (a la Churchill's description of democracy as the worst form of government apart from all the others). It is evil. Creative accountants have flourished under the auspices of multinationals eager for profit. How much more do we need their imagination in the service of God's kingdom where everyone who thirsts can come to the waters, where those without money can buy and eat, where the water of life is given freely as a gift (Isa 55; Rev 21 again)! We will turn to wealth and poverty in chapter 4. Here we focus on work and employment under the capitalist economic system. We are valued under this system not for who we are but for what we produce. Profit and economic growth are placed above everything else, over all systems of morality and any pretense of justice or peace. I have value in this society to the degree that I labor to produce wealth. Those who do not work for pay or do not produce wealth are by definition not valued. I have spent a long time in company with those with a dysfunctional relationship with paid employment, often incapable of work or unable to get it. They know that they are without value, cast out from society, disregarded and seen as either pitiable or scroungers on the rest. Is this the kingdom of God? It is crucial for the church to say to such people, to all people, that they are loved and valued simply for who they *are*: precious humans created in the image of God, graced with unique gifts and personalities that find their true expression in the kingdom.

It is interesting to note that the functional, profit-driven view of work that predominates ends up casting work as an enemy and a chore. For those in paid employment the goal is often the next weekend, the next holiday, the retirement (an odd concept justified nowhere in scripture). For some without work, so lost and futile in their thinking, work is something to be avoided at all costs. For both groups the assumption is that if we just had enough money—all our physical needs taken care of—then of course we would not work. You do not need to spend long in the company of those with no work, paid or unpaid, to realize that their minds, hearts, and souls are a fractured, aimless mess. We are valued simply for who we are but we are created to *work* in God's kingdom. For all the corrosive effects of the fall may tinge our labor with futility we who are part of the new creation should see work as joyful worship.

Work seen through the lens of God's kingdom issues a joyful summons to all those corroded and corrupted by the false economics of society. To those frantically laboring to produce wealth, toiling over some of the longest working hours in Western Europe, Jesus bids a gentle ceasing and offers a different rhythm (let alone what Jesus bids to the global structures where many outside North America and Europe toil in near-slavery in work that pays very little, precisely for the benefit of those in affluent nations!). To those whom society condemns as incapable or unwilling to work, vilified and demonised in their feckless derangement, Jesus calls to an active participation in the kingdom using their unique gifts. God's liberation subverts the idols of freedom, whether the freedom that disguises itself as endless toil or the freedom that is masked in an absence of purpose and responsibility. We are called to something so much better and the more the people of God model this subversive alternative the more a wondering, weary world will yearn to be invited in, to participate in the liberation we were created for (Matt 11:28–30).

This restoration of work to something more gentle and beautiful than society's competitive conception is in many ways dependent on another larger liberation: the liberation of time.[2] We belong to a Creator who knows how to rest. The institution of the Sabbath at creation was a holy event, reverenced week in and week out by God's people. They ceased from their labor and they rested. How we need to regain the holy wonder of rest in this frantic, frenzied age! God knows the meaning, the rhythm, the passage of time. "When the fullness of time had come . . . "(Gal 4:4). There is a new day dawning (Rom 13:12a), a new season, a whole new conception of time that bears the hallmarks of God's gentle reign of grace. We are invited to participate. It is ironic that a culture owing much to what was called a "Protestant work ethic" finds itself in need of such redemption.

When we rest in God we get our perspectives realigned, and this in turn gives shape and meaning to all our activity. We cease not because we can then do more but because there will be more life, more love, and more freedom in our doing. To cease does not mean that we miss out on the opportunity to do more, as in the fears of the popular imagination and the packed timetables of earnest Christians. To cease increases our capacity to love. It increases our capacity to see ourselves and one another in God's perspective. It increases our capacity to give ourselves wholly to God and others. The level of our activity becomes less, the number of our tasks reduces, but the quality of our lives is enriched and deepened. This is why the pattern, whether weekly or with some other regularity, is so important; it keeps us grounded. When I cease I remember that actually my work is not mine but God's. The world goes on without me; its burdens are not mine to bear. It does not all depend on me. I cease and am renewed. Work is both elevated and diminished in the Sabbath. Elevated, for it is seen as God's work that I am graciously invited into, an opportunity to see all my gifts and labors used in and for the kingdom. Diminished, for work is not an economic necessity or taskmaster, not a totalitarian despot whose whims I must obey and whose yoke I must always bear. Work isn't

2. On what follows see Stackhouse, *Day is Yours.*

even necessary for my sufficiency, my daily bread and clothing. God knows what I need. I am loved (Matt 6:8, 11; note the echoes of God's provision of daily manna in the Exodus wanderings and the clothes not wearing out from Deut 8:3–4). In the Sabbath all is brought into proper perspective again and I am restored. Too many churches and too many ministers have heaped heavier and heavier burdens upon their backs and the backs of others (Matt 23:4), denied the Sabbath, profaned the sacred season, and have stumbled in darkness rather than dare to walk in the light of God's new day, God's new time.

What forms of life and habits of mind and heart might enable us to enter into God's liberation of time, of work, of existence? Enable us to invite the broken like Bobby into something better than belief and to begin to treat one another and creation with peace and justice? There's a question for discipleship! This is what it means to work out our own salvation (Phil 2:12). There is a vision of mission and hope that lifts our eyes to the glorious dawn! We will return to some at least of these questions. The inheritance is assured and the land lies open before us by the Spirit. "If today you hear his voice, do not harden your hearts." (Ps 95:7–8; quoted throughout Heb 3–4, full of Exodus imagery and rest). There is a resurrection. We can begin to walk a different and a better way.

———•◦•———

This has been little more than suggestive of a richer, deeper, holistic view of salvation. There remains much more work to be done and much more to be said. I end with a story that has for years provoked me to question the meaning of salvation.

Simon was someone we knew at Graih. He was painfully withdrawn, monosyllabic at times, but always polite when he did speak. He only spoke a lot when under the influence of the substances he struggled with. There is a picture of him with a group of other guys in the mist and the rain of one of our ill-fated walks in the Manx hills. He's huddled over in a hoodie and he looks proud and happy. He was found dead in his boarding house room soon after a stint in prison. He was in his thirties. A lot of us from Graih attended his funeral. Afterward one of the volunteers turned to me and said, "He who receives you receives me." (Matt 10:40). This volunteer had taught Simon at school many years previously and she spoke about people not having the capacity to respond to Jesus, but to respond to his people. Simon knew nothing of faith, of hope, of love, knew nothing of Jesus or his kingdom, knew nothing of God's liberation. He had a broken spirit. He was under cruel slavery to beings that by nature are not gods, unable to hear the good news of liberation. But he knew some of God's people, and he knew their love for him, and he responded with as much kindness and gentleness as he had. "He who receives you . . . " Was this a response to Jesus? Does such a response of receptivity to the love of God's people carry something of salvation? Are Jesus' people such bearers of salvation, the light of the world, the Messiah's very body? If so, how does that change our self-conception, deepen our responsibility, ennoble our work and calling?

I have no answers. But I have enough questions to know that lives like Simon's are the hard edge of salvation in the real, broken, messy world. No simple solutions, abstract prayers, or comfy beliefs will do. Cheap grace redeems nobody, buys nothing. These lives and the desperate questions they pose cry out for a re-evaluation of salvation from a church that needs to unmask its idols of safe freedom and specious worship and rediscover the breadth, the height, the depth, and the glory of God's liberation that frees us to worship with all of our lives.

Chapter 3

The God of the Kingdom and the Idol of the State

The trees once went out to anoint a king over themselves. So they said to the olive tree, "Reign over us." The olive tree answered them, "Shall I stop producing my rich oil by which gods and mortals are honoured, and go to sway over the trees?" Then the trees said to the fig tree, "You come and reign over us." But the fig tee answered them, "Shall I stop producing my sweetness and my delicious fruit, and go to sway over the trees?" Then the trees said to the vine, "You come and reign over us." But the vine said to them, "Shall I stop producing my wine that cheers gods and mortals, and go to sway over the trees?" So all the trees said to the bramble, "You come and reign over us." And the bramble said to the trees, "If in good faith you are anointing me king over you, then come and take refuge in my shade; but if not, let fire come out of the bramble and devour the cedars of Lebanon."

—JUDGES 9:8–15

But our citizenship is in heaven, and it is from there that we are expecting a Saviour, the Lord Jesus Christ. He will transform the body of our humiliation so that it may be conformed to the body of his glory, by the power that also enables him to make all things subject to himself.

—PHILIPPIANS 3:20–21

THE PARABLE ABOUT THE trees is uttered by the sole survivor of a massacre in pursuit of power. This is yet another tale of the idolatry, tragedy, violence, and depravity—counterbalanced by the immense fidelity and patience of God's grace—that run as cycles through the book of Judges. Gideon, mighty savior of the people of God, has died (leaving behind him the bitter taste of a relapse into idolatry, Judg 8:22–28) and his son Abimelech has hired men to kill his brothers. Gideon's sons are slaughtered, but Jotham alone survives. He tells this parable (described as a "curse" at 9:57), and flees. By the end of the chapter, following more deceit and violence, Abimelech is dead. Such is how power acts, always. This is what the pursuit of power leads to, always. It didn't have to be this way.

God had rescued his people to be a holy possession, the bearers of his name among the nations, the means of blessing the whole world. The Torah is full of repeated pleas for holiness, for not following other gods, for not acting just like all the other nations around Israel who were supposed to learn from her what being truly human meant. Instead, Israel learns from the nations, succumbs to the conforming power of this age and seeks a figurehead, an institution, a politician for herself. Gideon had told the Israelites that he wouldn't rule them, God would (Judg 8:23). They refused to listen, and lauded Abimelech as king. Later Samuel was heartbroken as the people demanded a king (1 Sam 8:6–9). You can hear God's anguish there and in Hosea 11:1–4. Even in the midst of such rejection God is gracious enough to take the rebellion and idolatry encapsulated in the search for a king and use it as a vehicle for his own purposes. Through David and the royal line that followed, so tied up with the Temple and the promises of salvation, there is an ambivalence in the exercise of political power that so often degrades into violence, excess, and oppression. Jesus, living at a time full of expectation, political promise, and revolutionary violence, rejects the offer of Satan, whose ownership of the nations is not disputed (Luke 4:5–8). He goes on to tell his still-confused disciples that there is a very different sort of power at play here, not like the rest of the world (Luke 22:24–27). Even then Jesus' disciples break out into violence in Gethsemane and ask the risen Lord if now, at last, the kingdom was going to be restored (Luke 22:47–53; Acts 1:6). Paul writes to the Roman citizens in Philippi and tells them that they actually have another allegiance. Caesar is not Lord, nor Savior, nor God (all things ascribed to the emperor in the first century). Against the totalizing exercise of worldly political power there seems to stand a very different kingdom and a very different king. Does this mean that we can safely withdraw from all that messy, compromised politics? Sure of our own purity, can we render unto Caesar what belongs to him and focus instead on the spiritual kingdom?

Some years ago friends of mine decided to invite a homeless man to live with them. Percy was not only homeless but was also severely depressed, to the point where getting up from wherever he was lying took significant effort. My friends, seeking to share the burden that such need presented them with, invited another young man to live with them as well. Their hospitality, generosity, and sacrifice was immense as they embarked on a difficult journey, uncertain of the risks and the future. Questions, meals, boundaries, prayer, and discussions all took place in the small terraced house. Percy's motivation for anything, for life itself, was at a nadir and the love that my friends showed was hard and sacrificial and transforming. In the depths of such pain there are no easy answers and no neat solutions. My friends fought for access for Percy into the mental health service, they supported him through long and difficult treatment, and they continued to show love, patience, and grace as he moved into his own accommodation, returned to work, and began an amazing recovery.

Under a strange loophole in Manx legislation what my friends did was illegal at the time. It was against the law for four adults, two at least unrelated, to live together under the same roof. Whether they knew this at the outset or not, were they right to break the law in this way?

———◦•◦———

Christendom has gone.[1] The millennia-long marriage of church and state has fractured. The state, keen to free itself of religious pretensions (or so it thinks!), has forged its own secular path. The church, cuckolded, has often protested at its perceived marginalization, of the erosion of its power and influence. Some have welcomed what they see as a fresh freedom, in the ambivalent margins of an increasingly unequal society, to articulate new expressions of an ancient faith.[2]

The myth of the Christian nation was always just that: a myth. It was a pretty horrific myth as well. Pick any period of history after the first few centuries AD and you won't have to look far to find the church embroiled in violence, genocide, war, corruption, greed, perversity, slavery, and colonialism. Keen to keep her rights and privileges as the sole arbiter of truth, goodness, and salvation the church happily baptized the actions of the state. Power always seeks to protect itself, in contrast to Jesus, the exemplar of a power and a love that always seeks the good of the other. Even today, though they parrot the dying echoes of a disgraced creed, you hear people talk about the "Christian" country. This makes no sense. Individuals can follow and believe in Jesus; countries cannot. The following of Jesus demands a self-sacrificial love and a renunciation of power, both things that the state is incapable of doing. The

---

1. Some date its death as far back as the end of the First World War; Mac-Culloch, *History of Christianity*, 915. Suffice to say that its death-throes continue to be felt, while others either mourn or dispute its demise.

2. Kreider and Kreider, *Worship and Mission*; Murray, *Naked Anabaptist*.

equivalence between church and state was always and is always hubris.

There is another side to this coin. Part of the fracturing of the whole perverse notion of Christendom has come from the modernist project of banishing religion to the private sphere. Everyone can breathe a sigh of relief, one thinks, as the state gets on with the business of being the state and the church gets on with the business of being the church. The state governs the public sphere, administers justice, engages in diplomacy, taxes and protects its citizens. The church is concerned with "spiritual" affairs, the private soul of man and his postmortem destination, the abstract and eternal truth. The two can never and should never meet. This view of the world continues to exert huge influence over both church and state. Yet the church professes to follow a man who was hung on a cross for being just another failed revolutionary. The early church was accused of turning the world upside down (Acts 17:6) by proclaiming a different king to Caesar. Not really the actions of a group of people concerned only with a private spiritual relationship with God and the hope of heaven when they died.

Somewhere in the middle of this spectrum—either the church and state totally equated or totally divided—there comes the mass of people who just want to live their lives. "Of course we must obey the laws of the land," they say, "for doesn't scripture tell us to?" The very suggestion that the church might intentionally break the law is greeted with horror. We'd be no better than the criminals! At the very same time we also say that if we were ever told that it was illegal to be a Christian we would of course "obey God rather than man" (Acts 5:29) and continue to name Jesus as Lord. Christians in far-off lands where it is illegal to bear the name of Jesus are prayed for and supported, while we are careful to maintain our legal standing both as individuals and as an institution (we, heirs of the Christian nation, blessed by the right sort of government as opposed to the tyrannical oppression of those foreign parts).

What is missed in this context is an entirely different sort of threat. Why bother to make Christianity illegal when you can just stop people *acting* like Christians? It makes no odds to a smug secular government what beliefs people hold, what meetings they attend in their spare time, or who they name as an abstract lord, be it Jesus or Darth Vader. Who cares? Just make sure that you don't invite too many homeless people to live with you (that would breach environmental health law). Or look after the unwanted elderly and children of society without the state's oversight and regulation (that's the prerogative of the social services). Or educate people without the state's consent (we need to make sure you uphold "our values"). Or tend to the mad, the sick, the blind, the lame, and the prisoners without the permission and blessing (and often the dead hand of bureaucratic regulation) of the state. Christian belief need not be illegal as long as Christian praxis is.

When churches tear themselves apart in endless debates about how to ensure they stay on the right side of the law, especially when they refuse to *do* what is right in case of breaking the law, the state can smile. Its power is secure, and this Jesus they name as Lord obviously means nothing to them other than a hope for life after death. In fact, this isn't even a threat, certainly not in my context; it's a triumph. The highest good is equated with being legal, in a gross conflation of legality and morality, and the very state that has just robbed the church of her distinctive praxis is held up as a master to obey. The idols still hold sway. Under this model my friends should never have invited Percy in. They could have lobbied government for a change in the law, written to their elected representatives, gathered petitions, and prayed for the situation to change . . . but they shouldn't have invited Percy in. While the legislative behemoth writhed, of course, Percy may have died, or gone mad in one of the faeces-soaked doorways he collapsed in. But my friends would have stayed on the right side of the law, as all good Christian citizens should.

The absurdity of neglecting someone suffering for the sake of remaining legal gives us a window on to the root of the problem (James would have had harsh words for such neglect! 4:17). This has to do with our self-understanding. Are we citizens of the world or the kingdom? The fact is that we are invited to seek first the kingdom (Matt 6:33), from which all else will follow. It isn't the case that, as in so much Christian discourse, we obey the law up to the point where it conflicts with God's kingdom and then we disobey; the point is that we seek first the kingdom, strive for the justice and peace it embodies, and *in so doing* we may happen to obey the law of the land as well. We may not, and this conflict should neither dismay nor deter us.

There is nothing intrinsically good about the law. What is legal is a very different sort of question from what is good. The legal powers of the state—the mass of jurisprudence that supports a vast host of judges, lawyers, magistrates, and courts—simply has no bearing on God's kingdom. Paul at least seems to have something very different in mind for the church in 1 Corinthians 6, where he tells the church not only that they will judge angels (and much else besides) but reacts with horror at the thought of Christians going to law against one another. We are citizens of something better and truer. We follow a different king, one whose precepts aren't dependent on the shifting cultural context, legal precedent, or the interests of the powerful. We obey someone else. We belong not under the power of darkness but in the kingdom of the beloved son (Col 1:13). To concern ourselves with legality is to miss the point, to get our priorities the wrong way round. Strive first for the kingdom.

The nation state, itself a very modern concept that needs to be looked at critically and that we need not accept, is not part of the new creation, the world where God will be all in all. If it is not part of the new creation why lavish upon it time, devotion, and service? Why bother to participate in something that is passing away? Like those ordering their lives by the old covenant in Hebrews 8 we grope after "a sketch and a shadow" when the permanent lies before us. We should be clear that this does not absolve us of political action and agitation, lest by this dichotomy we lapse again into the false antitheses of governments running the earth while the church is concerned only with "heaven." Justice and peace are political realities. In the face of the state—controlled by the powerful and always self-interested—they are realities that will bring the church into political conflict. But the kingdom of God is political in a very different sort of way to the pompous preening of the politicians of this age.

Following from the radical difference in our self-understanding as a people of a different king and kingdom there flow three areas where we confront the idol of the state: allegiance, violence, and hope.

First, allegiance. The state demands obedience from its citizens in every area of life. Its very cohesion depends on this obedience, from the payment of taxes to the provision of police services. The state requires that we conform. It has always been thus. Power, in whatever age and in whatever form, seeks obedience from those under its sway. Its own insecurity craves the legitimization that comes from such obedience. In the first century what we might call political life was inseparable from religious concerns (and social ones, business interests, civic duties, and so on). The fastest-growing religion in Asia Minor and the near East was the Caesar-cult, where the emperor was deified and worshiped. This political master was described in inscriptions as a savior, a son of god, the lord of the known world, the one who brought salvation and peace to all under his sway. This was called the gospel, the good news and the royal announcement of Caesar. To live life as a citizen under his sway meant paying him "religious" homage, attending feasts and sacrifices in his honor, and holding civic positions like priesthoods. Conform to this pattern and you will do well. To disobey . . . well, that usually meant rows and rows of Roman crosses. The peace and security of the empire were bought by the sword.

It was into such a situation—into the very heart of the empire!—that Paul dared to write about a different gospel, another Lord, a real Savior, and urged people not to be conformed (Rom 1:1–5, 16–17; 12:1–2). This would come at an immense cost, for to refuse to name Caesar as Lord was to cut yourself off from all the avenues of power and position and change. How would the Christians ever be able to influence the world if they isolated themselves in this way? To intentionally divest yourself of the very means of change seems poor advice for a political campaign of justice and peace.

The ways of power in the twenty-first century are the same. The gospel of democracy has rung out from the West as a cry of freedom. It is the highest good that cannot be questioned. It is legitimated through the obedience of the voters, or their supine indifference. From a Christian perspective there's nothing inherently good about democracy. All it means, in theory if not in practice, is the rule of the people. Christians tend not to dwell too much on the fact that their faith declares all people slaves under the power of sin, darkened in their senseless minds and futile in their thinking (Rom 1:21), in need of the light of Jesus. If people are that messed up, why ask them to govern? When the state then takes the obedience of its citizens and engages in all sorts of idolatrous activity, from war to rampant economic greed and environmental devastation, why pretend that we have to participate in this monstrosity? This holds true whether the state in question is democratic, tyrannical, oligarchic, or whatever. They are all under the power of sin. They are all idolatrous. They all demand from us, and govern by, an obedience that we as Christians cannot and must not give. We must refuse to legitimize this idol. This difference of allegiance is what lies behind the Christian practice of vote-spoiling, of refusing to hand obedience to the powers and giving them the pretense that they can govern in our name. It is also what informs Christian anarchy.[3] Anarchy is a much-misunderstood term. It does not mean chaos, despite being often tarred with this meaning. It means "no ruler." No democracy, no tyranny, no legitimizing the powers, no bowing to the idols. No king but God.

Second, violence. The state governs through violence. Always. It was Hobbes who pointed out that the threat of the sword lies beneath every social, political, and interpersonal relationship.[4] That seems an accurate enough description of a life, and a society, lived in servitude to the idols of power and the state. If you do not conform to the state's demand for obedience you are punished with the sword. You are forcibly brought by the police to the courts, who then forcibly impose their judgment upon you and

3. Ellul, *Anarchy and Christianity*.
4. Quoted in Brimlow, "What about Hitler?" 55.

may deprive you of liberty. All this is supported by the coercive power of violence. This is obvious. As citizens who conform we tend to think that this violence is a good thing, for we keep the law and the sword is there to punish the wrongdoer. The early church knew differently, and were urged to continue to do what was right regardless of the consequences (1 Pet 2–4). Violence is the foundation of the state. In contrast to this the kingdom of God is radically non-violent. Blessed are the peacemakers. Turn your cheek. Give your cloak. Love your enemies. Pray for those who persecute you. Overcome evil with good. (Matt 5:9, 39–48; Rom 12:21). The state, any form of state, *by its very nature*, cannot do this or condone it. Social cohesion depends on people not acting in this way. If they did, the world would be turned upside down. The kingdom of God was instituted and embodied by the one who refused obedience to the powers but gave faithful obedience to the Father, a self-emptying obedience leading to slavery and death (Phil 2:5–11). This is a costly kingdom, but it is where our true identity and humanity are found.

The threat of violence and the practice of violence creates an atmosphere of fear that pervades every aspect of our lives, and this fear is manipulated by the state and the powers to reinforce the status quo. We need to be afraid of the stranger rather than seeing them as a blessing, or even as Jesus (Matt 25:31–46). We need to be afraid of those who will take our position, our rights, our possessions, not see these things as gifts to be given to those in need (an important point when we consider the Christian's social position and context; those with nothing have nothing to fear). We need to be afraid of those who can take our liberty and enforce their will upon us, not see them as slaves to a shallow boasting that has no hold over us. Again and again throughout scripture, and especially in the NT, we find God pleading with us to stop being afraid. The Christian life, in its paradoxical freedom and joy in the face of oppression and suffering, is the fearless life. We are loved. Love never fails. Perfect love casts out all fear (1 Cor 13; 1 John 4).

Violence lies not only at the heart of the state's own life and functioning but inevitably spills over into international relations.

The perverse moniker "defense ministry" for the institution of state aggression is endemic, and idolatrous. How could the church be so seduced by this brutality? In spite of mass compromise and often collusion with the sword Christians throughout the ages have been at the forefront of non-violent demonstration and action. Whether it is blockading arms factories or camping on the streets civil disobedience continues to lead to violent repression by the state, wherever you live. Yet costly praxis and the prayer that it informs must be at the core of discipleship. We follow the one who loved and who refused the temptation of violence.

There are some spectacular successes won through non-violent civil disobedience, and there are even more ongoing battles and failures. The motive for Christians engaged in this area is resistance to the powers but, at a deeper level, faithfulness to Jesus regardless of "success."[5] We are invited to share the Messiah's sufferings. The NT is full of an anarchic community that is founded on selfless love for one another, a love found not through human effort but by the Spirit. They name a different lord and seem to have a maturity in dealing with division and conflict in their own community (Matt 18; Acts 5,15; 1 Cor 6) without recourse to the state or the powers. They suffer and they love their enemies. The early church was known for its refusal to not only bear arms but to hold any civic office that involved power over another (magistrates, for example). They would not participate in the violence of the state at any level and they bore the exclusion and suffering that brought. Under such circumstances their praxis of love amazed and terrified people by turns, and the church grew (Acts 5:13–14). Today it is inconceivable that we would give our cloak as well if our coat was demanded of us (Matt 5:40); that we would rather be defrauded by a brother or sister than to go to law against them (1 Cor 6:1–8); that we would refuse to call upon the state-sanctioned violence of the police. To offer alternatives is difficult and requires massive courage and imagination. There have been amazing experiments in non-violent community "policing" in remote

5. Brimlow, "What about Hitler?" 56–59.

Mennonite communities in South America.[6] This is no charter for political quietism or withdrawal. This is the invitation to pick up your cross, to go through the waters into a new humanity, and to begin to order our life together in relationships of love and not violence. The bloodied idol of the state has no place here. We give no allegiance to those who wield the sword.

Third, hope. This is the most seductive aspect of the idol of the state: the promise that it can bring change. This hope is what enlivens the politics of this age. This hope is what is held out to citizens, especially in democratic states. You want to change the world? Go into politics. You want to see sweeping social reform, equality, economic growth, peace, security, and stability (insert your favorite slogan here)? Vote for me. We conform to this hope whenever we lapse into the belief that the state really can bring about the change we want to see. To give the state this function is to demean the one who is the way, the truth, and the life. The good, the ultimate good, is found in the kingdom. The kingdom is never to be equated with a state, regardless of the state's form. That was the blasphemy of Christendom. Untold amounts of hope, of energy, of thought, passion, time, and gifts have been poured into politics in the tragically mistaken belief that it will bring about the longed-for utopia, or even take a baby step towards it. History is littered with the frayed remnants of these projects that held up so much promise and delivered so little.

There is even more at stake here, though, than such mistaken aspirations. When Christians cede to the state the sole capacity to enact the good we rob ourselves of being the bearers of such change. The light of the world meekly hands her torch to another. The questions of our life together, of the civic space, of justice and peace are all given over to the state, with its confused legislation and inherent violence. A slur often leveled at those who refuse to vote or spoil their vote is one of apathy; the precise opposite is the case. The apathetic, the unfeeling, are those who relinquish their responsibility to embody and enact change *themselves* and instead look to the faceless, violent state. We "vote" every single day by the

6. Schlabach, "Christian Pacifists Reject?" 67–68.

actions we take and the world we therefore seek to create. We are always in the process of becoming somebody, both as individuals and as a body.

The church, free of the idol of the state and unfettered by the belief that the state is needed to enact the good, can get on with the far more important—and fundamentally *political*—task of participating in the kingdom.[7] The questions of how we deal with violence and conflict; how we order our life together; the nature of authority and credibility; the role of decision-making; and who we live with and spend time with are all political questions that God is intensely interested in. They are also questions that can be asked and answered *without reference* to the state. It simply isn't needed. To focus on the state, or to believe in its ability to bring about lasting change, is to put our faith in something that is passing away and is crumbling into dust. The temporary has passed; the permanent is here. The kingdom is here. The political task lies before us, it is urgent, and it is on a wholly different foundation than the power-plays, pretensions, and posturing of the state (Eph 2:19–22). There is no king but God, and the good is found in his kingdom. To live otherwise is to be content with an idol's rule.

What, then, about the state? What about the scriptural passages that seem to enjoin submission to the state? What about the good that the state does seem to achieve? All that has thus far been said about the state has been from the church's perspective. It is part of the Christian faith that the summons to obedience sounds out to all, and that we are slaves without the liberating act of God. The state still has some function in a world full of those who do not profess Jesus as Lord. The only anarchy that is acceptable is Christian anarchy, founded on the self-giving love of Jesus. Any other sort of anarchy (and strictly speaking, from a Christian perspective there can be no such thing, for without God we are enslaved to rulers whether we acknowledge it or not) leaves the strong in power over the weak, where those with the most force rule. Of course, it is crucial to note that this is absolutely no different from the current

7. On the church and politics see Claiborne and Haw, *Jesus for President*.

"democratic" context, hopelessly co-opted by the vested interests of the powerful.

The Christian faith declares the radical brokenness of all and the need for a radical change in our lives, so radical that it can be spoken of as new creation. Apart from this new creation there is darkness, decay, and death: the rule of the idols. At its best the state may provide some sort of stability and limited protection in this slavery (what you need is liberation though, not a nicer slave-master). Here is where the church can and should call the state to account and encourage it to enact as much justice and peace *as it is capable of*, while recognizing that it cannot ever bring about the justice and peace of the kingdom. There is a place for the church to challenge the state towards something better even as she denies it the ability to fully reach it. This may seem like having our cake and eating it, standing outside the state but calling it to act justly, but such is the scriptural witness.

There are beautiful passages in the Johannine literature that speak of a relationship with the world founded on faithfulness to God rather than the demeaning patterns of the nations, not escaping such realities but seeking to transform them. Jesus speaks throughout John 13–17 of not belonging to the world but he does not ask God to take his disciples out of the world. The ultimate invitation is never to be a better state, but to give up the idolatry and find liberation. We do not participate in, need, or agree with the state, but neither do we attack it or seek to overthrow it. Our priority is always the kingdom. This perspective is less about the state and more about the church (lest we fall again into the trap of focusing on the state too much). We are called to embody an alternative political reality, with all that that entails. The mission and responsibility of the church thus widens and it becomes incumbent upon her to embody the hope, the peace, and the whole-hearted allegiance to one Lord that she proclaims. If history tells the sad story of the misguided hopes placed in the state then it also tells the tragedy of the church failing to be the church and turning her back on her birthright and responsibility. It is this shouldering of responsibility to *be* the good, this taking up of the cross, that ensures that the church's political life and claims can never be arrogant or triumphalistic. We know our broken inconsistencies too well for that. We tread a fragile, narrow path, following the one who emptied himself for the sake of love and bore what needed to be borne. All of the church's life and witness flows from the paradoxical power of the humiliating cross. There are no false slogans or easy promises here, but there is a love that is deeper and more real—and capable of bringing true change and life—than the sophistry of the idols.

In faithfulness to Jesus the church also submits to the state. Romans 13:1–7 is the most famous passage in the NT, alongside others, used as a defense of conformity to the state. Of course, Paul mentions nothing about different forms of the state so presumably the advocates of conformity would as happily obey a totalitarian regime like Hitler's as the supposed democracy of the contemporary UK. Paul was writing into a fraught context of competing claims for allegiance, peace, and hope. There would be many who would want to use revolutionary—even holy—violence to bring about the reign of this new king called Jesus. Paul and others wanted to stop such misguided compromise with the powers. New Christians had to see that the kingdom was a very different sort of kingdom than Caesar's. To fight would be to admit defeat, and return to the realm of the idols. To even go to law against one another was already a defeat (1 Cor 6:7). It is also a different thing to obey than to submit. I can submit to you without obeying you. The state can make its laws and wield its sword but the church focuses on the good regardless of legality; she will not fight. Like Jesus going to the cross, we submit. There may be crosses to be borne, fines to pay, floggings to take, prisons to endure, even death, but we cannot help but follow our King, for love. We will not obey if you ask us to stop doing good, but we will not violently resist you if you want to force your will upon us. We will submit. The letter of 1 Peter is perhaps one of the more stirring and beautiful invitations to such a difficult, costly, yet powerful life. Church history is full of those who refused to obey evil but also refused to fight, and who paid a high cost for their faithfulness. In all of this we seek first the kingdom.

Paul also wrote into a world where the claims of Caesar were total in every respect: religious, political, economic, and social. Caesar was god, and required consequent worship and obedience. To state, as in Romans 13:1, that all authorities are under the God revealed in and as Jesus is to severely demote, dethrone, and relativise the tyrant. A whole host of NT passages are invoked here, from the soaring heights of Eph 1–3, 1 Cor 1–2 and Col 1–3 to the brilliant response of Jesus to those who sought to trap him (Mark 12:17). The injunction to give to Caesar what is Caesar's sounds like a pragmatic compromise to those not soaked in the radical nature of scriptural faith. It is interpreted by the cry of the psalmist: "The earth is the LORD's and all that it is in it." (Ps 24:1). If all of creation is God's Caesar finds himself with nothing, with his haughty boasts reduced to so much empty posturing before the true King. When we follow Jesus we have no need to bend the knee to anyone else. We cannot serve two masters. We were bought at a price. We belong to another. Our citizenship is in heaven, whose life we now live in the crumbling remains of the state and the world's politics of coercive violence.

As the church reclaims the anarchic nature of her life in a fallen world ruled by the powers she finds that the state is but one of those mysterious forces that influence broken humanity. Ephesians 6 is Paul's classic exposition of struggle against the "principalities and powers" but many of the passages quoted above refer to these "dominions", these "rulers." There is a fractured, rebellious, dehumanizing, and debased power behind so much of our pain, our wounds, and our world. The violence, allegiance, and seduction offered by the state is but one example.[8]

There is a spirituality behind the most mundane actions and forms of life that we are called to recognize and resist. These can

8. Ellul, *Subversion of Christianity; Meaning of the City*. Ellul was a prophetic and powerful voice exposing the powers both in his sociological and theological works. A comprehensive overview of Ellul's life and thought is found in Goddard, *Living the Word*.

be the massive sociopolitical constructs of entrenched power , corrupt corporate interests, and oppressive economics or they can be the dynamics of the tiny church committee. Anyone who has sat on a committee can witness to the fact that there is more at play than the sum total of its participants. There is an organizational spirituality that can very easily crush people's lives and suborn what can be mature, loving Christian discourse into a pattern of loveless and abstract decision-making. If we cannot recognize and resist these powers we lie helpless before them. We need not spend our lives forever second-guessing ourselves or seeing dark spiritual forces in every cranny but neither should we bumble along in a hopelessly blind and conformed ignorance, believing that everything will turn out all right because we've said a quick prayer. We need to have the joy and the life, the creativity and the courage, to embody the alternative (Rom 12:1–2). The victory has been won (Col 2:15); we have the incredible honor of showing a groaning world what that victory looks like.

There are myriad ways the powers seek to influence our lives, and thus myriad ways to resist. We can but offer some brief suggestions. The realm of story is a particularly powerful way to shape how we view the world, each other, and ourselves. In the age of mass media there are all sorts of stories on offer. We are saturated by them. The state tells a story of democracy, of human rights, of morality and legality in opposition to the tyranny of the "terrorists" and the foreign dictators. This story demands that the state have arms to protect itself (and spread "freedom", "peace" and "democracy", as well as assuaging its citizens' fears and offering "security"), and the police and security services need ever more power. Behind this story is the familiar one of redemptive violence. This story is everywhere, from the state to the books we read and the films we watch. Violence gets results, it says. There are bad guys out there with guns. We're the good guys (of course!), so we need more guns to make sure the bad guys get defeated and we (or peace, or freedom, or democracy, or security) win. We *need* violence. The NT suggests otherwise (1 Thess 5:3). It should not take much reflection upon Jesus and his kingdom to see how anti-human (and therefore anti-God) this story is. From the television shows titillating us with the promise of instant riches or fame to the advertisements telling their own powerful story of how to look and what we need our mental space and spiritual life are colonized by the powers. The computer games we play offer an escapism where we can believe in a safe world we can control and understand (and often thus participate in "safe" violence where we can start again if we die). Our education system deifies results and qualifications, without which you are worthless.

All of these stories have a common factor: fear. Fear of not appearing a certain way, or having certain things, or the "enemy" out there that we need protection from, or the prospects we won't have if we don't get that exam result. These stories thrive on terror. These are the powerful tales that shape us, not just as individuals but as a society. They are, to use an emotive term, demonic. There is nothing intrinsically wrong with computer games, or film, or organized education (although I think a good case can be made against television *as a medium* regardless of content) but, as with all human endeavor and indeed all creation, apart from Jesus they lose all meaning and begin to devalue us, seeking to rule us, shape us, and eventually kill us. God loves our creativity in learning and media and all aspects of human culture, but these are servants and not masters. They need redeemed. They offer us something they cannot give. Life is found in Jesus; all other paths are death.

To these powers a holistic discipleship must be brought. We are in need of transformation. It is absurd to think that a daily quiet time, a homegroup meeting, and a Sunday service will do anything much against the onslaught of the powers. Five minutes of scripture reading won't do much in the face of hours of television. The stories we fill ourselves with matter immensely, for they will shape our unconscious assumptions about the way the world is. The ongoing joy of the Christian life is discovering and working out the way we *really* are, growing into our new humanity, working out our salvation, dreaming the dreams of the kingdom. The story of God, of creation and his purposes for it, is magnificent. It subverts, confronts, and reduces the powers and the tales they peddle.

The church inhabits a story of intimate love and cosmic grandeur; we are invited to live such lives. It is time to wake up (Rom 13:11) and to live, understanding the world we live in and embodying, in all of our lives, alone and together, an alternative story. A new creation. Paul, writing to the urbane and worldly Corinthians, in an astonishing evocation of Israel's bedrock of self-understanding (Deut 6:4–9) said that despite all the idols and their power plays there was "one God, the Father, from whom are all things and for whom we exist, and one Lord, Jesus Christ, through whom are all things and through whom we exist." (1 Cor 8:6). This kingdom, and this alone, we are called to inhabit, to turn from the death-dealing powers and find our humanity and our life. This is our glorious inheritance.

One of the most distressing signs of the rule of the powers is seen in Graih's drop-in. Many of those coming through the doors suffer from chronic substance addiction and complex mental health problems. Their lives—along with their minds, bodies, and souls—are a mess and for the most part they know it. All the joys of human life, from intimate relationships to meaningful work or activity, are stripped away.

Stanley has been coming to the drop-in for years. In the midst of addiction and mental ill health he has lost the capacity to respond differently to life. Once, when he had requested something from the drop-in and I had agreed to give it to him, he launched into a bizarre and frantic avowal of sobriety. This was as the fumes of alcohol rolled off him. When I managed to get a word in I told him that his sobriety didn't matter to me at that point but that if he continued to lie to me I wouldn't be handing anything out. Stanley couldn't stop himself. The lying that he relies on to manipulate his way through a society that despises him has become so deep-rooted that he cannot cease even when his lies are robbing him of the thing he wants. All the work of the powers eventually turn upon those ruled by them. The end is death.

The guys at the drop-in also exhibit an amazing and deep-rooted commitment to looking a certain way. Designer clothes, trainers, hats, and phones carry huge weight. It could be that, devoid of any other dignity or control in their lives, the guys reach for what they can. I think it goes deeper. There is something awful about a life that has such emptiness, pain, and death at its heart desperately trying to live up to society's expectations of how to look and what to possess. It is a literal shell, and just as brittle. A whitewashed tomb. Broken spirits and a cruel slavery. These are lives under the thumb of the powers. They are extreme examples but they point, like all marginal situations do, to the rotten core of mainstream cultural values and the more easily masked peccadilloes of the "normal."

It is worth noting, in particular reference to the power of the state, that the guys are also disproportionately affected by the legal powers of the day. These fragile, fractured lives are often consigned to prison or fined. They are dragged before the courts for strings of petty and pathetic offenses, and punished accordingly. Rehabilitation or reintegration into society is a myth for the guys. Contrast these lives subsisting at the bottom of society with those flourishing at the top. There are no long criminal records or prison sentences for financiers who have caused far greater misery around the globe than the guys are capable of. There are no punishments meted out on deceitful bankers and traders who have fixed market rates, defrauded the taxpayers, and pocketed their bonuses.[9] The state, corrupt and corrupting, chooses instead to vilify those who already have so little, while allowing and even encouraging the rapacious behavior of those who have so much.

Alongside such allegiance to the powers, oppression by the powers, and a belief in a certain story the guys at Graih regularly exhibit *the* characteristic of the powers: hopelessness. The nihilism and despair weighs down lives and minds who cannot dare to believe that their existence, or the world, could ever be different. "Just listen to the news; everything is getting worse." "Let us eat

---

9. Fines for institutions do not count. Individual bankers and traders are unaffected and beyond liability, a luxury not afforded to the guys.

and drink, for tomorrow we die." (1 Cor 15:32). This is a closed-down prison of existence. This is hell. The Christian response to this, as Paul puts it in 1 Corinthians 15, is resurrection. There's a real King, and the petty despots better step aside. There's a real story, and the deceitful lies we tarry with better shut up. There's a real hope, and the pathetic pretensions of appearance, possessions, and prestige better stop their prattling. Only when we give whole-hearted allegiance to the King and dare to live in the freedom of the new and yet ancient story of scripture can the church embody an alternative to those ruled by the powers. This is the citizenship of heaven, and when we inhabit it we partake of glory.

Chapter 4

The God of Poverty and the Idol of Wealth

Mortal, make known to Jerusalem her abominations . . . I pledged myself to you and entered into a covenant with you, says the Lord GOD, and you became mine . . . Therefore, O whore, hear the word of the LORD . . . As I live, says the Lord GOD, your sister Sodom and her daughters have not done as you and your daughters have done. This was the guilt of your sister Sodom: she and her daughters had pride, excess of food, and prosperous ease, but did not aid the poor and needy . . . So be ashamed, you also, and bear your disgrace, for you have made your sisters appear righteous.

—EZEK 16:2, 8B, 35, 48–49, 52B

For you know the grace of our Lord Jesus Christ, that though he was rich, yet for your sakes he became poor, so that by his poverty you might become rich . . . For if the eagerness is there, the gift is acceptable according to what one has—not according to what one does not have. I do not mean that there should be relief for others and pressure on you, but it is a question of a fair balance between your present abundance and their need, so that their abundance may be for your need, in order that there may be a fair balance. As it is written, 'The one who had much did not have too much, and the one who had little did not have too little.'

—2 COR 8:9, 12–15

When a man strips another of his clothes, he is called a thief. Should not a man who has the power to clothe the naked but does not do so be called the same? The bread in your larder belongs to the hungry. The cloak in your wardrobe belongs to the naked. The shoes you allow to rot belong to the barefoot. The money in your vaults belongs to the destitute. You do injustice to every person whom you could help but do not.

—BASIL THE GREAT (c. 330–379 AD)

It is not from your own property that you give to the poor. Rather, you make return from what is theirs. For what has been given as common for the use of all, you have appropriated for yourself alone. The earth belongs to all, not to the rich. Therefore you are paying a debt, not bestowing a gift.

—AMBROSE OF MILAN (c. 340–397 AD)

EZEKIEL, BROKENHEARTED, UNPOPULAR, AND extreme, utters a lurid diatribe against the chronic unfaithfulness of Israel. Despite God's love and compassion his people, his bride, have turned away, rejected the covenant, sought other lovers, and engaged in the worst forms of adultery and sin. In the midst of this Ezekiel brings up Sodom, ever since Genesis held up as a paradigm of corrupt humanity, and declares that Israel's sins have made even Sodom appear righteous. And the sin of Sodom? Not the debauchery and sexual perversion associated with it in the popular mind. The sin of Sodom was her refusal to aid the poor and needy while amassing wealth, prosperous ease, and excess of food for herself. Israel has done even worse things than this.

The fate of the poor, the needy, the orphans, the widows, and the alien is a constant theme in scripture. Ezekiel's sorrow and rage are not unique. The prophets are unanimous in their denunciation of the plight of the poor. Isaiah 1 is programmatic (and again links Jerusalem with Sodom). Isaiah 58 puts justice for the poor above "religious" observance (even those enjoined by Torah). Jeremiah 7 denounces the Temple, pleads for justice, and rages over the house of God's name becoming a "den of robbers" (used many years later by another prophet, raging again at the religious institutions while the poor were neglected and oppressed). Hosea 2 is an anguished plea for Israel to turn from seeking wealth and prosperity in themselves and instead be found by God "in righteousness and in justice, in steadfast love, and in mercy." Amos 5 declares God's hatred for the very festivals and worship Torah asked for in the absence of justice to the poor. Micah 2 rages at those who covet possessions and oppress the poor. Habakkuk 2 puts wealth, called "treacherous" by the prophet, at the heart of Israel's imminent destruction, with the very walls of the houses built by injustice testifying against the people. In Zephaniah 3 the rich are those full of pride while the poor, lame, and humble will be vindicated by God. In Zechariah 7 Israel's refusal to render true judgments, to show kindness and mercy, and not oppress the poor is the reason why she is exiled. In Malachi 3 the priests are rebuked for, among other things, oppressing the widow and the orphan.

The poor are not just central to the prophetic canon. The Torah is full of stipulations protecting the marginalized, often with the reminder that Israel herself was a poor slave in Egypt before God's act of liberation (Exod 22:21–27; Lev 19:9–10, 33–34; Deut 6 warns about forgetting this when enjoying the wealth of the promised land). Deuteronomy 15 and Leviticus 25 are full of radical economics that bring together the poor, forgiveness of debts, and acknowledgment that all we have is God's. In the histories wealth is tied to oppression (see the people's request for a king in 1 Samuel 8). Through 1 Kings 10 and 11 we see Solomon's descent into apostasy, explicitly tied to his phenomenal prosperity. The psalms speak often of wealth and poverty (Pss 4, 9, 10, 12, 14, 15,

22, 34, 37, 40, 41, 44, 49, 52, 55, 58, 62, 68, 70, 72, 73, 76, 82, 94, 102, 103, 107, 109, 112, 113, 119, 132, 138, 140, 145, 146, 147).

The NT opens with Mary's Magnificat (Luke 1:46–55), echoing Hannah in 1 Samuel 2 and many Psalms, singing of the rich being sent away empty while the hungry are filled with good things. Jesus quotes Isaiah 61 at Luke 4:18–20, at the start of his public life. The poor are "blessed" (Matt 5; Luke 6) while the rich find it hard to enter the kingdom (Matt 19:23). Jesus identifies himself with those on the margins (and we are then known by our *actions* towards him/them) in Matthew 25:31–46. In Acts 2 and 4 the early church are known for having "no needy among them" as they share all that they have. The epistles are full of exhortations to show love, hospitality, and generosity to those in need, culminating in James and 1 John tying the existence of faith to the practice of love for the needy. In the 2 Corinthians passage above Paul makes full use of both Jesus' example and the provision of manna in the Exodus to plead for an equality, a fair balance, of riches in the community of faith. Revelation 18 castigates the oppressive military, social, and economic power of Rome, living in luxury while trading human lives.

All of these passages are merely exemplary, pointing to a theme which is quite obviously present and often central throughout every time and genre in scripture. A full list or study is beyond our scope. They are cited here for two related reasons. First, to point to the centrality of the poor in scripture. In much scriptural, especially prophetic, thought the very existence of covenant faithfulness (or lack of it) is seen through behaviors towards the poor. Acting for justice for the poor and needy isn't an add-on to faith, a religious duty tacked on to some other core; faith constitutes such action. Second, this point is raised here because the suggestion that the poor are central to faith, in lots of ways, provokes immense controversy and hostility, often in the face of the overwhelming biblical witness. By seeing that scripture is neither silent nor neutral on issues of wealth and poverty we glimpse the fact that our attitudes are far more shaped by the patterns of this age. Although the church has been of, with, and for the poor at many times of renewal in her history she has also frequently been complicit in amassing wealth, oppressing the marginalized, and baptizing injustice. Perhaps it is no wonder that we remember Sodom for its sexual excess rather than its oppressive wealth (is there a link?). We continue to try and ignore the cry of the needy.

━━━◆━◆━━━

Trevor and Susan lived in one of the worst boarding houses. There are no minimum standards for such establishments in the Isle of Man, leaving vulnerable tenants at the mercy of a landlord's whim. Some landlords are fair; others are not. It is not rare to find people renting a small, damp room with nothing as secure as a written lease, no access to heating or hot water, no access to cooking or laundry facilities, no proper sanitation facilities, no locks on their door, and precious little hope. A strapline of the Manx government in recent times, eager to paint the island in attractive colors, has been "Freedom to Flourish." The question of who is free and and flourishing is perhaps germane to this chapter but we will not explore it here. Suffice to say that Trevor and Susan lived in an environment that degraded both their mental and physical health.

Trevor and Susan both suffered from chronic addictions and all the associated mental and physical problems. They were not uncommon, sharing similar traits with many who find themselves sunken or pushed to the bottom of society and left to die behind closed doors. The wall of their room was black with damp, the same damp that clung to what little possessions they had. The sink in the corner was broken. They had no bed, just a filthy and stinking mattress in the corner. They had no furniture and whenever I visited they were sat on the pock-marked carpet, surrounded by mounds of clothing, rubbish, and the odd poignant photograph of one or the other's children. They were deteriorating and they were desperate.

The response of the few agencies in contact with Trevor and Susan was to send quaint letters with appointments that neither of them could get to. Again, their situation could make an interesting case study of the shallow and pathetic response of institutional "specialist" agencies to such total depravity, but that is not our purpose here. What struck me most about Trevor and Susan—and never more so than when I visited them after a church meeting—was that they never would have considered approaching the church for help. Not because they were anti-Christian. Not because they were scared or distrustful of odd beliefs. Not because they would feel out of place. They were desperate. They would have gone anywhere and asked anyone for help. Approaching the church simply never crossed their minds as an option to consider. Why would it? That's not what the church is for. The distorted and truncated spheres of influence where the church looks after people's private, "spiritual" lives and charities or the state tend to the materially poor, sick, mad, and needy is shared across the Western Christian world with all those championing a new secularism. It never occurred to Trevor and Susan that the church would be even interested, let alone helpful, in their plight.

The sad thing, of course, is that they were right. Their ignorance of the church was matched by the church's ignorance of them. They remained out of sight, out of mind, and out of hope.

God is the God of the poor. In a unique way that no other group in any age or society possesses the poor *are* the people of God. In many of the Psalms attested above it is assumed that the poor are God's people, often oppressed and exploited by the wealthy. Israel spent much of her history as a small and fragile nation trampled on by the empires of the day. It's no surprise that Israel had her genesis in the liberation from the poverty of slavery. It's no surprise that the prophets engraved God's love for the poor and his thirst for justice into their witness. It's no surprise that Jesus spent time with the marginalized and that they were those most drawn to and affected by his embodied proclamation of the kingdom. It's no surprise that the early church strove to share all that they had and in mutual generosity sought to eliminate poverty (the parallels between Acts 4 and Deuteronomy 15 are many and would bear fruitful reflection on the church's newfound sense of entering into their inheritance, the "promised land" that was now the new creation where there would be "no more needy"). It's no surprise that in the immediate post-biblical period the pagan world looked on in astonishment at the bedraggled, persecuted Christians rescuing abandoned infants and caring for all those in need regardless of creed or background.

There are instances in scripture of wealth being tied to God's blessing or favor. Far more often, however, wealth is seen as something ambiguous and dangerous. In Genesis 13 the combined wealth of Abram and Lot meant that they had to part ways, a poignant symbol of the necessary division that wealth causes, even within a family. Wealth is tied with violence and oppression in the scriptural imagination, for wealth is acquired through violence and injustice and sustains the powerful who rely on violence to maintain their position. You don't find many poor rulers, in the ancient world or today. The example of Solomon was noted above. Less well known but perhaps even more tragic is the aftermath of Joseph's story in Genesis 47. Joseph uses his position of power not only to acquire immense wealth for himself and his family but then goes on to make slaves of the Egyptians in a horrific foretaste of the fate that will overtake his descendants. Wealth always protects itself, at any cost. Even when individuals are in positions of wealth (one thinks of Daniel, for example) they are there to witness to God (thus subordinating and relativising the pretensions of wealth and power) and preserve his people (thus taking the purposes of God, the story of faithfulness, forward). Wealth is never to be an end in itself. The only use it has is when it is poured out for others, as we see in the NT when rich women support Jesus (Luke 8:1–3) or when Lydia gives her house for the fledgling church (Acts 16:14–15).

The NT follows the OT pattern of denouncing wealth, from Jesus telling his disciples to sell everything and give to the poor, to the rich young ruler unable to yield his wealth, to how hard it is for the rich to enter God's kingdom (Luke 12:33, 18:18–25), all the way to James's rage at favoritism for the rich (Jas 2) and the death of Ananias and Sapphira as they sought to keep wealth for themselves (Acts 5). Wealth is an idol with a long history and an endless capacity to corrupt and entice. Or rather, mammon (that evocative term that goes beyond mere wealth to encompass the attitude of insatiable acquisitiveness) is the idol behind the false security and fake promises of wealth. It is well known that Jesus spoke more about money than almost any other subject. It would be nice if the churches that claim to bear his name imitated him in this, but unfortunately the mention of wealth has a deadening, silencing effect.

Poverty is complex. People can be poor in many ways, not just materially. Much is often made of the difference between Matthew's "blessed are the poor in spirit" (Matt 5) and Luke's more straightforward "blessed are the poor" (Luke 6), but this is unnecessary. The meaning and referents belong together. You tend to find that poverty is present at many levels within the same individual or community. The poor in spirit *are* the poor materially, and vice versa. Matthew's stress on the forgiveness of debts in the Lord's prayer (Matt 6) should leave us in no doubt of his economic concerns, as much as later Christian usage has "spiritualised" his words to more abstract "sins" or "trespasses." The complexity of poverty is in fact one of the main excuses people use to evade the challenge of the poor. "The rich may well be rich, and not poor, but they're poor in spirit and need us at their side to tell them the good news of Jesus." We are back in the bizarre world of Christian discourse that we looked at in chapter 2, where presumably some of us are called to be drug dealers and prostitutes so that we can reach people engaging in these activities. Paul was in no doubt: Jesus was poor, and that poverty brought in God's kingdom (2 Cor 8:9) and made us "rich." If Jesus had needed to be rich and powerful to reach those who were rich and powerful the Christian story would look very different. He didn't and neither should those who follow him. It might be a scandal and a stumbling block (1 Cor 1) but that's Jesus. The lie of "we need to be rich to reach the rich" is shown in the western church's sickening complicity in upholding systemic and individual structures of unjust wealth and rapacious acquisition at the cost of both creation and human life.

Context is more important in the discussion about poverty than anywhere else. My own context on the Isle of Man is inescapably affluent. As part of a privileged niche of the Minority World I enjoy a level of affluence and access to both basic necessities and luxuries that most of the rest of the world would find unimaginable. It has been estimated that we would need three planets to provide the resources for the current world population to enjoy my standard of life (in Paul's words, a fair balance). Even this is far behind the five planets needed to bring us all up to the average North American. In this context it takes significant effort to both seek out the local poor and to prevent the acquisition of further wealth. It is assumed that I will get richer as I get older, expected even (and the current economic malaise affecting my generation has done little to dent our perception that such a growing affluence is our birthright). It takes serious discipline to resist the trend of upward mobility, or to reverse it. I am one of the rich, not the poor. This brings a whole host of ambiguities to my thoughts. I have no answers.

The Isle of Man has made its money in recent decades by fostering an offshore financial system that targets the global elite, personal and corporate. The financial sector is responsible for a vast amount of jobs and prosperity, all of which depend on systemically unjust flows of capital from the poor places of the world to the rich, from the cash-strapped and tax-poor nations in the Majority World to the decorous wealth surrounding the armies of accountants and lawyers in tax havens and secrecy jurisdictions. A further blight on Manx life, and another damning indictment of anyone who claims that there's a "trickle down" effect of wealth, is the island's response to the poor of the world. The UN recommends that Minority World nations give a minimum of 0.7% of their annual GDP to foreign aid. Not a lot to ask of us who have made so much over the past few hundred years from the exploitation of the rest of the world still bearing the scars of empire. The Isle of Man manages, from its position as servicer of global wealth and a debt-free government, to give 0.06%. You would think that such a blatant travesty would enrage those steeped in the prophetic call that bellows from the pages of scripture, yet the churches of the island are strangely silent on this and most other economic issues. Perhaps our complicity—in our jobs, in our homes, in our patterns of spending—means that we are either blind or unable to heed the call for justice. Meekly we bow the knee, conform to society, and allow the idol of wealth its unalloyed rule.

The wider context between Minority and Majority Worlds is also important.[1] We are heirs of hundreds of years of colonialism and the systemic exploitation of creation. The global structures that govern our lives and societies have been set for a long time and they depend on fundamental inequality. The capitalism that we live and breathe—that we accept without complaint or critique, still less opposition or alternative—has at its very foundation the oppression and exploitation of the majority by the minority. It can be no other way, which is why attempts to reform the system are doomed. A more radical alternative is needed. The idol of wealth rests on a huge amount of power and has a smug smile of decadent complacence on its face.

When these contexts are borne in mind we are able to escape the comforting abstractions that dog this debate more than any other. It is crucial to remember the world we live in. This is one of the most important points that sharpens the discussion of poverty. It may be the case that in a world where everyone's basic needs are met it is possible to have people richer than others without oppression and injustice; but that is not the world we live in. It may be the case that in a world where everyone has enough to eat we need not be concerned about wasting half of our edible food, or using precious resources to support expensive meat-eating rather than basic necessities; but that is not the world we live in. It may be the case that in a world where no-one is exploited we can buy goods from across the earth without care for their usefulness or provenance; but that is not the world we live in. It may be the case that in a world where everyone has a family and a home we can live as individual family units in private houses shared with no-one

1. The classic study is Sider, *Rich Christians*. His prophetic call was first issued in the seventies and has not yet been fully heeded.

else; but that is not the world we live in. We could go on. Context matters.

And what a context it is. The disintegrated despair of Trevor and Susan is poverty on a local scale, the dark underbelly of an affluent society. The sheer numbers of those living and dying in poverty in the Majority World are just that: numbers. The statistics are as impersonal as they are overwhelming. From the rock-bottom life-expectancy of sub-Saharan nations to generational slavery in India; from Haitians eating cakes baked with mud and salt to the Bangladeshi clothing workers crushed at Rana Plaza. Boatloads of desperate, penniless, and exploited people sink as they attempt to get to more affluent shores. Rich nations do their best to try and exclude these terrified and uprooted people while the media portrays a nightmare scenario of "waves of migrants" that will sweep away life as we know it (comfortable, safe, quiet, and above all untouched by those urgent, needy poor people).

Even when we know about the chronic problems elsewhere we are rarely personally connected to them and often overwhelmed by the scale of the suffering. We turn off our television sets because the "news" depresses us. We get "compassion fatigue" from too many advertisements with photographs of starving children with their eyes begging for our money. As I write this the Ebola virus continues to ravage Western Africa. Thousands are dead, thousands more are expected. As the disease has raged this year the World Health Organization has decried the lack of investment into treating Ebola or researching a vaccine. One WHO official said, "The rich get excellent and expensive care while the poor are left to die." The Minority World looks on—for the most part unaffected and unworried despite some lone cases that have themselves engendered a frenzy of self-protection—as a virus that could be prevented from spreading within a reasonably good healthcare system claims more and more lives. Pharmaceutical companies are uninterested in developing a vaccine for a virus that affects poor people. There's not a lot of money in the West African nations; there's just a lot of death. It's another example of the systemic and unjust global structure that insulates the rich and leaves the poor to die after robbing them of the wealth of their countries. This is the world we live in. This is the context within which we must dare to articulate a Christian vision and hope. This is the real world, and it needs to change.

Abraham Heschel writes about a trait of the OT prophets that he calls "the importance of trivialities." "They make much ado about paltry things, lavishing excessive language upon trifling subjects. What if somewhere in ancient Palestine poor people have not been treated properly by the rich?"[2] What matter if there's a few thousand more orphans in Ebola's wake? Who cares if a couple of alkies die, diseased and alone in a dank room? Even a cursory flick through the Psalms provides an answer. "The needy shall not always be forgotten, nor the hope of the poor perish forever." (9:18). "'Because the poor are despoiled . . . I will now rise up', says the LORD." (12:5). "You would confound the plans of the poor, but the LORD is their refuge." (14:6). In a provocative collection of essays entitled "No Salvation Outside the Poor" Jon Sobrino called the current situation of poverty in the world the "sign of the times." "I am appalled to see that, apparently, no one is taking responsibility for the inhuman state of our world," he wrote.[3]

The fact and extent of poverty locally and globally is a reality that changes everything else. It must determine all our theological discourse and radically shape our individual and common life. It is a sign of the times that forms who we are in response to it. While there is one person going hungry, one child without proper healthcare, one worker in bonded slavery, one precious human being created in the image of God suffering we can be sure that God is lamenting and is yearning and working for justice, healing, and peace, giving his own life so that reconciliation may be won. The church is called to do no less. If we do not, we cease to be the church.

To all of this need, this utter and abject horror, we come in the humility of faith, hope, and love. Rather than turning away, overwhelmed or guilty, we need to glimpse Jesus and we need to stay

2. Heschel, *Prophets*, 3.
3. Sobrino, *No Salvation*, xii.

close to him. From very early on the church understood the para-doxical nature of their crucified King and the need to follow him. Philippians 2:5–11 finds Paul urging the church to have the same mind as Jesus, who gave up every conceivable wealth to become an obedient slave. Paul models this himself, as he reminds the Corin-thians, becoming poor so that others may be rich, imitating Jesus himself (2 Cor 6:1–11, foreshadowing 8:9). We are urged to imitate the God revealed in and through Jesus (1 Cor 11:1; Eph 5:1–2). Jesus provides us with a model of relationships of love (Rom 15:7). Peter, writing into a context of suffering, tells the church that it was to this we are called, following Jesus (1 Pet 2:21). Here, indeed, belong all those soaring passages in the epistles about being "in Christ", about growing into fullness and maturity in Jesus, about participating in the very life of God. This isn't abstract language idly reflecting on supposed theological or metaphysical truth, this is language about what we do with our mundane, daily lives and how they can carry the very glory of God. This is about the way we walk, and it's a walk into poverty, into death, precisely so that the new life of the kingdom can be seen and won.

If Jesus is to be identified with the poor and marginalized (Matt 25:31–46) then that is where the church must be found. If Jesus knew and feasted with the despised of his society (Mark 2:15–17) then that is what the church must be known for. If Jesus saw the kingdom of God in terms of the prophetic vision of justice and peace (Luke 4:18–19, quoting Isa 61:1–2 and alluding to the great forgiveness of debts in the Jubilee of Lev 25) then that is what the church must proclaim and live. It is important to note that the church cannot simply *serve* the poor; that would breed paternal-ism. The church must *be* the poor. It is only when the church joins the poor, as the poor, in the struggle for peace and justice that the kingdom is glimpsed. This is the tragedy of the affluent church, happy to give money to a "mission" to the poor but never having either the love or the courage to become poor. We are like the rich man, asking Jesus about eternal life but unwilling to pay the cost (Mark 10:17–22). Or the Pharisees, happy to tithe even the herbs in their garden but neglecting peace and justice (Matt 23:23–24).

How many sermons on tithing do we hear? And we struggle even with that! It's a practice that Jesus nowhere commends. He invites us instead to take up a cross (Mark 8:34–38), to sell all that we have (Luke 12:32–34) and to be unworried and joyful as we do so. Who knows? We may even discover that in the vulnerability of poverty and the interdependence it forces upon us we find ourselves to be richer than we can now imagine (Mark 10:28–31).

In Jesus we see the cost of the kingdom.[4] The cross is the place of desolation and torture, of human existence forsaken by God and without hope. From the cross comes the cry of despair, brokenhearted and in anguish. It is to this place that Jesus went. It is to this place, these places, that the church must follow. The cost is always death. The cross was a place of forsakenness but going there was an act of love and obedience and the path of love and obedience still requires a renunciation, sometimes of our very lives but certainly of all our possessions and our gifts. There are crucifixions aplenty in this broken world. Cries of inchoate despair are still sounding out from the forsaken places of our planet. Where is the church? We are invited to take faith to the darkest and most desperate places of humanity. That is where God is, even if we seem to be forsaken. On the other side of death—whisper this transcendent hope—there is a resurrection. We come not with brash certainty and triumphalism but in anguish, yearning and aching for the kingdom. This is why the church must always be poor. Our vocation is to be the slaves of the world, the slaves in poverty making many rich. This is the narrow path that our King walks and which we follow (Matt 7:13–14). This is why Jesus spoke about counting the cost (Luke 14:25–33, a passage ending with an explicit command to give up all our possessions). To love, with all the vulnerability and fragility and hope that this entails, is to be willing to lay down our lives (Rom 5; 1 John 4).

What a transformation would occur if we took Jesus' words seriously and set out in fearful yet joyful obedience! What a difference if the church was known for its self-giving generosity in every way, if she embodied the Jubilee where there is no debt, if she

4. See Bonhoeffer, *Cost of Discipleship*.

willingly and lovingly welcomed people into her homes through adoption and fostering, if she was at the forefront of the call for justice in global systems, if she was always to be found amongst the precious poor and shared their sorrows and their hopes, if she was willing to give everything she had to make others rich! This isn't abrogating the responsibilities of governments and charities to provide for the vulnerable, but it is insisting that only the church can give her very life for those she seeks to serve and love. There is a context of slavery that is uniquely Christian, that only the church can fulfill with love and joy, the same love and joy she sees and knows in her King, the same love and joy she shares through the Spirit. In Romans 12, expounding what it means to be "living sacrifices" and have "transformed minds", Paul goes on to list the importance of love, followed by the exhortation to "associate with the lowly"; that is where the church must always be found. The church should be able to dwell at the poorest places of the world in a way that no-one else can. Only the church can give everything to see the kingdom come, to see the poor made whole, to embody justice and peace, and therefore to enter into her own salvation.

It is axiomatic in scripture that when God acts to bring salvation he will bring justice and peace for the poor (whose very existence in a creation of abundance is a fact of injustice). Read any of the Psalms, and remember that they have been the prayerful lifeblood of God's people through history. In this sense salvation cannot be outside the poor, for their existence is something that salvation will address as of central concern. The matter goes deeper than this though. There is no salvation outside the poor but there is also no God outside the poor. The problem of theodicy is not one of abstract formulations but of the poor, of the reality of suffering and injustice and oppression. The existence of the poor is a constant threat to the reputation but also the very reality of God. If the poor continue in their miserable existence then what can be said about God? Words fall silent before the horror. That is why the poor are of such concern to God. That is why the church must have no needy in her midst. That is why we must give everything to see the kingdom come. God, in an astonishing act of vulnerability, has not only thrown his lot in with the poor but has entrusted the embodiment of peace and justice to his people, who share his life through the Spirit (again we hear the language about the "body of Christ"). Israel was meant to be the light of the world (Isa 49:6; Acts 13:47) but the nations blasphemed God instead when they saw the idolatry of his people (Rom 2:24). As the people of the Messiah, the reality towards which Israel was always pointing, we are called "light of the world" (Matt 5:14–16). Do the nations blaspheme God because they see our idolatry? The poor are the responsibility of the church. To bring an end to the suffering and pain and horror and despair is the responsibility of the church. If we cannot even take stumbling steps towards this then we must cease to speak of God. If there is no salvation for the poor there is no salvation for any of us. If there is no God of the poor then there is no God.

In the poor we find a powerful and undeniable critique of the status quo. The poor are truth embodied. In the desperate, addicted loneliness of the boarding houses we see the truth of our fragile, selfish insistence on individual family units and homes. We see our lack of generosity and hospitality. In the systemic poverty of the Majority World we see the truth of the oppression and power of the banks and corporations that use our complicity to sustain unjust financial systems that allow the status quo to go unchallenged and unchanged. In the diseased, dying children we see the truth of our thirst for security and health at any cost, willing to bomb distant countries and take all the resources we can for our own sakes. In the ravaged countries, exploited and devastated for commodities, we see the truth behind our consumerism, our materialism, our hardness of heart. Like an icon we must hold the poor always before us, share their life and their struggle, to remind us of what is at stake in our lives. Before such truth we are helpless. We can either ignore it, as the majority of us do, or we can give our lives to change it; we cannot deny it.

It is inconceivable the the western church (the most resourced, affluent, supposedly powerful church in history) continues to turn a blind eye to the suffering in our world, both on our doorsteps and further afield. For too long the lie of "what matters is that my heart is right before God" has been unchallenged. Jesus had harsh words for those who thought, even sincerely, that their hearts could be right before God in the absence of justice and peace. Instead of trusting ourselves to make those judgments we must listen to Jesus, who told us to look where the treasure is (Matt 6:21) to know where our hearts are. Our treasure is stored in banks funding poverty around the globe. It's stored in the bizarre mass of "Christian" merchandise, most of it produced in the Majority World for the spiritualised consumption of the Minority. It's stored in the buildings we love to lavish time and care and money on while the poor starve, or our safe homes while the lonely, needy, and mad suffer on our streets. The poor point to the pathetic pretensions of capitalism as a viable economic model, and to the need to articulate a different way of arranging our economy so that there may be a "fair balance." It is in this sense that the poor are prophetic, showing us the things that society tries to hide or ignore but that go deeper than the norms we conform to. When the church joins in this silent blindness, this willful ignorance, she stands self-condemned and the God she believes in is no God at all.

Staying close to the poor, becoming poor, is hard. It costs in lots of ways. Most current models of alleviating global poverty operate on the assumption of us ("the rich") helping them ("the poor"). And, indeed, the burden of change is on ourselves. We don't have three planets to play with. We haven't made a great fist of the one we've got. But rarely do we find contexts where we allow ourselves to be shaped, challenged, encouraged, and blessed by the poor. Yet this is the "fair balance" Paul urges. It is crucial to flourishing mission and discipleship that the poor are placed at the center of our lives, not tacked on as an optional extra "mission", not reduced to some donations on a bank statement. We need to build relationships of love. We need to know one another's names, share one another's food, joys, homes, hopes, and prayers. This needs to be done locally (somewhat easier, you would think, until the idea is suggested; it's easier to love people a long way away you never have to meet) and globally in networks of churches and long-term relationships and understanding. One major step is to renounce our wealth and become poorer.

I am still amazed at the incomprehension and hostility that mention of poverty or becoming poorer can bring from those who profess to follow Jesus. The sheer weight of scriptural evidence, the horrors of our current context, and injunctions from the very lips of Jesus can yet be set aside as too extreme, impractical, or dangerous. If the status quo is so obviously broken (and it would be a brave soul who would claim that we're all heading in the right direction) why does it still elicit such passionate defense? That is how powerful this idol is. Even conversation about money makes us uncomfortable. Try suggesting some financial accountability in your homegroup through mutual sharing of bank statements and see how many people volunteer. We are terrified of money. Again, scripture tells us this is no surprise. Wealth breeds fear: fear of losing it, fear of having less, fear of it being taken from us, fear of someone else having more. Fear breeds violence: we need to protect our wealth through force, we need to lock up our possessions and our selves from others. Violence brings only death and isolation. The west faces a crisis of people having so much and yet being so terrified and miserable. Wealth is always linked to fear and violence. To step away from it is to enter into liberation. Jesus in Matthew 6 speaks of treasure that cannot rust or be stolen, about a life free from fear and worry. The early church spoke of their treasure being found in the bellies of the hungry. When we have little, or nothing, we need not curl up in self-protective fear, terrified that someone will take it (a thief, "the market", or whatever). There's precious little to take. If they want it, they can have it (Matt 5:38–42). Here is a joyous life and love found in Jesus, a poverty that indeed makes us and others rich, a security in the love of God where there is no fear (1 John 4:18).

Poverty also brings massive credibility. In a society ruled by mammon people are suspicious of the church simply wanting to hoard money and resources for itself, and are amazed when we renounce what we have. Cultures have long memories and we should not be so isolated in our individualism that we pretend we are immune from the effect of long centuries when the church was rich, powerful, and oppressive. In many ways she still is. There is a lot of renouncing to do. Trust and hopes so broken take a long time to heal. Society will need a lot of convincing that the church means what she says when she talks about justice and peace and poverty. We can only begin to take humble, repentant steps. We cannot reach the rich by being rich, but we can both challenge them and show them a joyful alternative by being poor (which is what Jesus did). Poverty, both personal and corporate, brings undeniable authority and credibility, things that the church desperately needs. Our motives can be seen more clearly as love and a desire for justice when we are seen as not seeking profit. Our current context makes it a missional priority to be poor.

And how then do we survive? We bear one another's burdens (Gal 6:2). About this we will speak more in the next chapter. Wealth is there to be given away; that is its only purpose. True life is found elsewhere.

———

Blackie came to Graih as a thin, bedraggled, confused man. His alcoholism was steadily stripping his life of everything. Fellow drinkers used to congregate in his flat for binges, during which Blackie would often get beaten. He used to turn up to the drop-in limping, with dark circles round his eyes. People would urge him to take another path, to stop letting people in, to change his company. Blackie would shrug and smile and wince and the same thing would happen again, and again. His ever-cheerful outlook belied his immense vulnerability.

When Blackie's drinking robbed him of the last dregs of physical health he went into hospital and was then moved into a residential home, despite being in his fifties. The life-expectancy for guys like Blackie hovers around the mid- to late-fifties. We helped move his possessions from his semi-derelict flat, trying to pick out what we could from the chaos and storing it in bin bags for him. Amongst the detritus were some cards and photographs from his estranged family. One read, "To the World's Best Grandad."

Blackie's drinking didn't stop. He was kicked out of the residential home and ended up in a room in a boarding house. Once again we helped move his stuff, now reduced to a few bin bags of clothes that we carried up to his room that had nothing but a mattress in it. Blackie was found dead in that room. He'd been dead for some days when he was found by someone looking for a drink. It transpired that a few days before he died he'd had a particularly bad beating. It seemed that his frail body and mind hadn't had the capacity, or possibly the desire, to recover and continue.

At the end of all things I think it will be the likes of Blackie we will be most ashamed to face. It won't be our secret sins that accuse us before the throne of God, it will be the ravaged faces of those we could have loved and turned away from. When we cease to feel the rage and sorrow that lives—and deaths—like Blackie's should produce then we have lost hope. When we leave such wrecks to die we leave Jesus to die, re-crucifying the Lord of life and denying the one we claim to love and follow.

The Blackie's of this world, and situations far worse, are absolutely the responsibility of the church. If we have no faith, hope, or love to bring to Blackie then we have nothing. If salvation doesn't touch Blackie then it doesn't touch any of us. There is a cry of despair and horror at the tragic, inhuman existence of such poverty.

And there is a rumor of a better kingdom and a resurrection.

Chapter 5

The God of Community and the Idol of the Individual

> You have seen what I did to the Egyptians, and how I bore you on eagles' wings and brought you to myself. Now therefore, if you obey my voice and keep my covenant, you shall be my treasured possession out of all the peoples. Indeed, the whole earth is mine, but you shall be for me a priestly kingdom and a holy nation.
>
> —Exodus 19:4–6a

For we are what he has made us, created in Christ Jesus for good works, which God prepared beforehand to be our way of life . . . So then you are no longer strangers and aliens, but you are citizens with the saints and also members of the household of God, built upon the foundation of the apostles and prophets, with Christ Jesus himself as the cornerstone. In him the whole structure is joined together and grows into a holy temple in the Lord; in whom you also are built together spiritually into a dwelling-place for God . . . So that through the church the

> wisdom of God in its many colours might now be made known
> to the rulers and authorities in the heavenly places.
>
> —EPHESIANS 2:10, 19–22, 3:10

THE CALL OF GOD is the call to community. From the earliest times it was always thus, from the foundational calling of Abram in order that God might make him a nation and the whole world would be blessed (Gen 12:1–3). Israel always understood herself as a people, a family, a nation, not an unconnected group of individuals. God's call and purposes were bound up with Israel *as a community* far more than with individual Israelites. Even when individuals were called (from Abram to Joseph, Esther to Isaiah) it was to a vocation that had the community of Israel as its central focus, in creation, protection, or challenge.

And Israel's call was always for the wider, watching world. As the liberated slaves made their way through the desert to Sinai God reminded them of why he had called them. They were to be a kingdom of priests and a holy nation. In their sacramental role they were to be a light to the world (Isa 49:6), the bearers of God's redemptive purposes in the groaning creation. They were to show, by the peace and justice of their common life, what God always intended human community to look like (Deut 4:6–8). The early Christians, believing that Israel's purpose had been fulfilled in Jesus the Messiah and that the Abrahamic blessing was now flowing to all nations and creation, picked up on passages like these. Peter writes about the Christians being built into a spiritual house, that they are a chosen race, a royal priesthood, the creation of God, and all of this is not for the sake of the Christians but for the watching world, that although they may detest the Christians they are unable to deny their good deeds and thus glorify God (1 Pet 2).

Paul, throughout Ephesians 2 and 3, founds everything on Jesus. The church is the creation of Jesus, in Jesus, for the purpose of walking in a particular way of life that will make known to all authorities what the glorious wisdom of God looks like. More than that, the church is itself the very dwelling-place of God, the people through whom the divine life and love and glory of God are incarnate in the midst of a creation being made new. There could not be a higher view of the church, or of the Messiah whose body she is. The connections between a way of life, the dwelling-place of God, and consequent witness to authorities and powers have been present throughout this work and here in Ephesians they receive full and glorious expression.

It seems that the call of God into community transforms the individual, taking her up into a whole much greater than the sum of its parts. There is something crucial about the costly relationships of love that define and sustain such a community; something that witnesses to the very life of God. This has little to do with individuals and their own private spirituality or relationship to God. It has everything to do with the creation of a community that embodies God's purposes of justice and peace. The community, rather than the individual, becomes the primary lens through which we discern the kingdom of God. The community, rather than the individual, becomes the foundational way of understanding and entering into God's kingdom.

———◆———

Mark had already beaten his addiction to heroin. The low point had been a trip from the Isle of Man to the UK where he almost died of an overdose and had to be brought back by the friend he was with. Mark had leapt from the frying-pan of smack into the fire of alcohol, and he was getting consumed. Occasional work in the building trade and a serious relationship had both come to an end, precipitating a swift decline into a boarding house and the near-permanent state of inebriated, deadened confusion that is so familiar at Graih's drop-in.

Mark had come out of another short stint in prison and found himself once again at the very bottom: no possessions, nowhere to live, nothing to do but find some cider and someone to drink it with. While he was looking for a room in a boarding house he stayed in a squat, and it was here that he was sexually assaulted by a drinking partner. The first we knew about it was when Mark turned up at the drop-in and broke down. The police were called, statements were taken, and an investigation launched. We were left with Mark, alone and frightened and confused.

We needed to get Mark somewhere safe to stay, preferably away from the other guys frequenting the drop-in who wouldn't be helpful at a time of such vulnerability. What Mark desperately needed was people around him, people to care for him, to tend to him, and to give him some sense of stability when everything else was falling apart. At a church service, with Mark's permission, we shared his predicament with the congregation and asked for help.

Unfortunately no-one had the capacity to house and care for Mark. The extreme nature of his chronic problems and acute situation, the sheer depth of his need, was too much to bear for individuals and families with busy lives and busy concerns. Instead of a welcome into a place of safety we gave Mark some money and put him in a bed and breakfast. Alone. Instead of a family we gave him charity, and the pious assurance of our prayers at this difficult time.

As in many situations like Mark's, with testimony confused by substances and the victims concerned inarticulate and powerless, the police investigation came to nothing. Whatever scars or pains Mark bears are still deadened by the alcohol that is killing his body, mind, and spirit but may be providing the refuge that the community of faith found itself unable to offer.

———◆———

The individual, understood as possessing inalienable rights and ultimate prerogative, lies beneath and behind all the idols we have thus far considered. The deification of the individual (understood in terms of the individual being the center and arbiter of all things rather than the proper Christian "deification" whereby we partake of the life of God, becoming conformed to the image of the Messiah) has been the beating heart of our society for at least the past two hundred and fifty years. It is perhaps no coincidence that this has occurred as extractive capitalism and unfettered urbanization has spread across the globe. It wasn't always this way. It doesn't need to be this way.

The fact that I as an individual have the freedom, the right, and the authority to dictate the terms of my own life is assumed throughout the western world. It continues to provide the driving force behind the growth of societies in terms of economic achievement, politics, religion, and cultural expansion. As with so much else, the church has been swept along unresisting and unreflective. The very heart of Christianity has become "my relationship with God." Jesus died for me. He bore my sins. The very purpose of Jesus was this death for me. Jesus' death has now brought me to God. I will go to heaven when I die. The praxis of my faith (which is always personal and individual) is found primarily in my private devotions: my prayer life, my reading of scripture, my spiritual journey. I go to services where I can "worship" God in songs almost exclusively couched in terms of my singular response (we sing "I" not "we"). At these services I am fed, nurtured, cared for, valued, and included. I also get a chance to share my gifts, to discern my unique purpose and calling, to practice my ministry. This all brings me closer to Jesus, strengthening the personal, individual relationship at the center of my faith. If these services or that congregation aren't meeting my needs, recognizing my gifts, or catering to my preferences I go elsewhere, where I can find greater satisfaction (and nothing so exhibits our demeaned ecclesiology like the ease with which we move from one congregation to another, ditching one "family" for another). My faith, my calling, my salvation, my hope, my life, my spirituality all remain utterly mine, along with my God. All of these have me where I should be: at the center. Everything else gains its value and meaning from me.

There are some whispering voices that demur at the centrality of the individual. These, happily enough, can be ignored or squashed. Often they are denigrated as nostalgic, those wistful (often older) voices speaking of the breakdown of the community or the family. The pace and volume of individualism tramples all such feeble opposition, as the number of single households continues to explode and each person knows that wealth, health, and happiness are theirs by right, even if it has to be theirs alone and no-one else's. The individual's rights and dreams, their upward trajectory to success and prosperity, are the indisputable highest good even as wider society recognizes the fractures. Mental health problems touch one in four people. Loneliness kills more people than most other diseases. The moralists wring their hands at the vacuity of the acquisitive thirst of popular culture, with endless sparkly entertainment prancing across our screens while we grasp sleek gadgets in increasingly chubby hands. I can be the person I want to be, renewing and reshaping myself as often as I wish (with the help of all those clothes and possessions that are designed to express my very essence and are not at all manipulating my greed and vanity). I have a story of success. I have a dream and the world is there to help me realize it. I define my world. I am great. I am.

This may seem a caricature. No serious, thinking person could possibly agree that such an elevation of the individual could be a good thing, you say. Everyone knows it's relationships that really matter. Or at the very least, the church knows this in the face of an individualized society. They know that what matters is their love for one another. In fact, it is this love that defines them (John 13:35). Perhaps. It is always good to be proved wrong. But, as in all things, we must look at the praxis rather than listen to the words. If it is relationships of mutual love that define the church as followers of Jesus then we must look at the practice of her common life.

This is where the poor, again, provide a devastating critique that cannot be answered. In one simple, brutal stroke Mark's story—and so many others like it—expose the paucity of our common life. The community of love, with all its houses and spare rooms and stocked cupboards, does not have the capacity to welcome one who is homeless. The community of love, with all its language of belonging and healing and hope, cannot welcome one who is abused and broken. We are exposed as having no depth. All our services, our private devotions, our individual relationships with God, our songs, and our spiritual journeys are exposed as lacking that one defining factor: love (1 Cor 13). We do a lot of things. We create a lot of noise. We have a lot of resources. And one abused, homeless addict steps into our lives and there is silence. That is the power of the poor. They expose us for who we really are, and who we really follow.

There are, of course, exceptions to this. There are people of immense love who open their lives and homes and tables to the weakest and weirdest. I have been privileged to know some of those exceptions; their love continues to be a blessing and a challenge to me. The existence of such exceptions, however, only highlights the fact that they *are* exceptions. By their brightness they make the rest of us only darker, curtailed by the shriveled horizons of our own egos. The general trend and the normal expectations are relentlessly individual.

We should be clear as to why this is, before we fall into paroxysms of guilt. In fact, such a recourse to individual guilt ("I'm such a bad Christian!") is only the other side of individualism. There's just as much egocentrism in decrying our own sinfulness as there is in elevating our own desires. The monomaniacal insistence on my individual sin (which is, of course, all God really cares about because Jesus died for *me*) is corrosive and destructive when it fails to take anything else into account. We may be gods or devils but as long as we remain the center and goal of our universe we're radically out of balance. No, an increased individual guilt for this state of affairs will not help. There are individual factors at play and we should indeed grieve over our own hardness of heart, but we must lift up our eyes. Individualism is an idol, with all the weak but real power that idols possess.

The wider factors of society and its assumptions shape us not just as individuals but as congregations and communities. In many ways this failure of capacity to love and welcome those most in need is a failure of how we order our life together far more than a failure of individual love. There were, no doubt, many people who would have responded in love to Mark, but their circumstances meant they could not. Isolated in individual houses, these almost-lovers lacked the capacity to act on what they knew was right. It's too much of a risk taking Mark home. What about my children? I'm out working all day. I don't have time. I'm going away soon. I don't know what to say. We should note how much the lens of the individual continues to determine how we even formulate possible responses. Our very imagination is in bondage to the individual.

Before we go on to addressing this problem of capacity, of the lack of room in our lives, we need to take a step back. We need to recall why community matters so much, particularly the community of the church, as opposed to the individual. It will be helpful to recall the material we surveyed when considering salvation in chapter 2. There we saw God acting in liberation on behalf of a people, rescuing Israel from the slavery of Egypt and taking her to himself *as a people*. God's liberation is not only on behalf of a community, for the sake of a community, but that liberation is only a foretaste of God's larger plan to redeem and renew all things, so that he might be all in all (1 Cor 15:28). A scriptural view of salvation will always relativise and challenge our preoccupation with the individual. God is in the process of saving all of creation, not just me. In sharp contrast to individual testimony ("tell me how you came to Jesus and got saved") we find ourselves swept into something grander. I open scripture and find that, breathtakingly, God is not so much part of my story as I am part of God's story. My own salvation, as important as that is, only finds its place within a greater salvation. Jesus did not just die for me but in him God was reconciling all things to himself, things in heaven and on earth (Col 1:20). Not only am I a new creation, but new creation itself has broken into the cosmos and one day will be brought to completion (2 Cor 5:17; Rev 21–22). God, or creation, does not revolve around me. I revolve around God.[1] Baptism and the eucharist, those two great markers of God's people, are just that: markers of a community, a family, a body. They are far more statements about who we are together than they are individual affairs. Indeed, one of the sad ironies of many communion services is the rather morose focus on my own individual sinfulness at the very time when I'm supposed to be sharing in one loaf as part of one body. Community definition comes before individual spirituality. By taking this perspective we do not lose anything that an individual

1. Wright, *Justification*, 7.

focus sought to maintain (individual salvation, relationship with God, and forgiveness of sins) but we gain so much more. We gain a liberation from the enslavement of individualism. We gain greater meaning and value by being part of God's bigger perspective, of being individuals within his family and his story.

This is why the church matters. It isn't just that she's known as belonging to Jesus by the love of her common life (John 13:35). It is because she *is*, as a community rather than as individuals, the body of the Messiah, Jesus. The church's life is the life of God, with all that then means for witness to the wider world. The church is never totally equated with Jesus (he remains "the head", "the cornerstone") but she is his body. That is what Paul is hammering out in passages like 1 Corinthians 12 and Ephesians 2 and 3. People have been baptized, brought into, a new community (more, a whole new sort of humanity [1 Cor 10:32]!) and they are now members of the Messiah. The church is the living, visible, tangible proclamation and embodiment of God's wisdom. Through her, God proclaims to the world, to the idols, to the authorities and powers his victory of love. Through her, God continues to enact the justice and peace of his kingdom. Scripture aches with the beauty, frustration, hope, longing, fear but above all *importance* of the community of faith. It is this *community* that is the outpost of the kingdom. This *community* the recipient of and witness to salvation. This *community* that is God's body. Nowhere, in any of this, do we find the reductive individualism that has blighted our discipleship, warped our mission, and denuded the already frail threads of our supposed common life. We were made for more than ourselves.

To the shrill insistence on individual rights and freedom we find the scandalous testimony of those shaped by Jesus. We have seen how slippery the language of freedom is. Humans in self-imposed bondage to idols cling to the rhetoric of freedom and self-expression, desperate to ward off the falling dark. The fruit is seen in the chronic insecurity and fear that lies at the heart not only of ourselves but of society. For all our faux self-assurance we are terrified of ourselves, and will fill our lives with a considerable amount of activity and noise to avoid facing that truth. Paul's words seem harsh, but we are indeed slaves of whomever or whatever we obey (Rom 6:16). True freedom is found only where the Spirit of the Lord is (2 Cor 3:17), when the light shines in the darkness to give the knowledge of the glory of God in the face of Jesus the Messiah (2 Cor 4:6). Freedom is found in Jesus, a paradoxical freedom that involves us becoming slaves of one another as we engage in the costly yet joyful praxis of love (Gal 5:13). We follow the example of our Lord, in dying to ourselves and being raised into a new sort of life, a new sort of existence that is radically communal rather than individual, a new sort of freedom found in the slavery of love.

It is the same case with rights. Jesus was quite clear that the authority of the kingdom is based on humble service (Luke 22:24–27) rather than any conception of rights. Philippians 2:1–11 stands yet again as a central and powerful reminder of Jesus' own path of self-giving love and slavery, introduced by Paul's plea to the church to imitate the Messiah and consider others better than themselves. Jesus had all rights, and gave them up. It is the same for the individual and the community that follows him. Paul spends much of 1 Corinthians 8–10 discussing Christian freedom, including his own rights, and concluding that love transcends these. Paul talks of his own vocation in terms of a debt, becoming a slave to all for the sake of the gospel. He has just pleaded with the Corinthians to give up their own rights rather than go to court against one another, even to the extent of being defrauded (1 Cor 6:7), and he will remind them that they are not their own; they were bought with a price (1 Cor 6:19–20). Here indeed is a neglected sense of the "redemption" that Jesus bought for us! Far from assuring us of a private salvation and a heavenly reward Jesus redeems us into a slavery of love where we are no longer our own. We have no rights (I speak only of the church).[2] We belong to the Lord, totally. My dreams, gifts, hopes, desires, ambitions, fears . . . everything is now under Jesus. We sing as much but the practical effects are often a simple baptizing of our self-centered lives as we glorify the God

2. A powerful perspective on this theme is Williamson, *Have We No Right?*

who "plans to prosper us." The example of Jesus, Paul, and the early church knows otherwise, bound as they were to give up all rights. As one body we stand or fall, hurt or heal, rejoice or mourn (1 Cor 12:25–26). This is another compelling reason for the poverty of Christians. We are the people who uphold the rights of others but do not insist on them for ourselves. The context of the church must be one of being poor and making many rich. We give up all things for the opportunity to love and serve not only one another but the world. 2 Corinthians 6:1–11 is Paul's passionate exposition of just this following of Jesus: giving up all things as slaves of God for the sake of love. In all of this we do nothing but follow the one who loved us and gave himself for us (Gal 2:20).

What, then, of walking in this way? What do we do with the lack of capacity to love that is so evident in the fragility of our common life? What practical steps must be taken as we step away from ourselves and towards others?

The creation of community, the fostering of relationships of love, is simple. Simple, but very difficult. It is rooted in the sharing of life. The more we share life, the more the Spirit can bring that community and love that is always a grace and never a solely human construct. Bonhoeffer wrote, "Christian brotherhood is not an ideal which we must realise; it is rather a reality created by God in which we may participate."[3] To the same degree, the more we live separate lives the more we deny the Spirit the opportunity to do his work among us and through us. There is a spectrum of shared life and we are able, at any point, to either move closer to one another or to withdraw from one another. Discipleship consists of responding to the Spirit's invitation to choose love over suspicion, to choose mutual vulnerability over safe silence, to choose interdependence over self-sufficiency. We must recognize the importance of this even as we recognize the immense difficulty and hurt often involved as wounded people seek to come together. To die to ourselves is no easy task, yet as with the pangs of labor there is an exhilarating new life on the other side.

---

3. Bonhoeffer, *Life Together*, 18.

Ron Sider has a beautiful phrase that should echo through all exploration of a common life: "unconditional availability to and unlimited liability for other sisters and brothers."[4] The common life of the church must model this. Unconditional availability because our lives are open to each other, in time as much as in all else. Our hearts and homes are not ours, but they belong to the wider body, as we ourselves do. We are not our own. We will give time and attention and love to one another. Our wallets are open, too. To even raise the prospect of shared finances remains culturally taboo, as we saw in the last chapter. Yet it is precisely because money carries such symbolic weight in this culture that sharing it becomes a powerful symbol of one family. Our money is not our own, it belongs to the family. We must pay one another's debts and share one another's financial burdens because by doing so we proclaim that we are members of *one body*, a community rather than a collection of separate individuals with separate lives who only overlap on scarce shared activities (a Sunday service, for example). Someone once asked me, as we discussed the kingdom, who would send his children to university if he gave up his affluent job to join something better but lower-paid. The answer: we will. The church will, if we can. Either way, we trust in the God who asks us to dare to seek the kingdom first, who knows what we need and invites us to live without fear or worry (Matt 6:25–34). Too often the implicit assumption beneath our individual lives is that we'll serve God and the kingdom when everything else is sorted out, as an added extra to the cultural symbols of a mortgage, a career, a university education, good holidays, possessions . . . the list goes on. The common life of unconditional availability and unlimited liability is scarier but truer.

If participating in a common life is a spectrum we start at one end: living together. This seems extreme to so many but this is only because we have normalized the pathological desire to have individual households. You don't have to go far back in human history (or look at many other contemporary societies) to find the extended family playing a far greater role than today, let alone

4. Sider, *Rich Christians*, 164.

tribal or clan affiliations. The nuclear family is a modern construct based on a level of prosperity largely achieved through oppression (how ironic that this truncated family unit bears the same moniker as the most destructive force we have created). There are degrees of living together, too. You don't have to look to the great monastic orders or radical modern equivalents such as the Bruderhof[5], The Simple Way[6] or the Catholic Worker movement[7] to discover Christians sharing houses and lives. A common life at its richest has a common house, common meals, common prayer, and common work, but sometimes only one or two of these elements are present as people attempt to live and walk together.[8]

The more we share the more we build interdependence rather than independence. "Independent living" remains the slogan that dominates health, homelessness, and addiction discourse. I've always found it nonsensical. No-one really lives independently, and it is puzzling that anyone would want to do such a thing. To live my life independently of others seems prideful, arrogant, and profoundly lonely. It is a life shorn of the deep and intimate relationships that in their mutual vulnerability make human life worth living. In fact, the myth of independent living is one of the factors that have caused people to have problems in the first place. All it breeds is loneliness and fear: the products of idols. It makes no sense to just patch people up and send them back out to the war to get slaughtered. You need to make peace and stop the wounds happening in the first place. Interestingly, most rehabs for substance abuse have all the elements in common referred to above (for common prayer read "spirituality").[9] Is it any wonder people struggle so much to return to "independent" living? It just condemns people to a certain sort of Sisyphean hell, forever striving

5. www.bruderhof.com/en, and see their public statement of their common life in *Foundations*.

6. www.thesimpleway.org

7. www.catholicworker.org

8. See the discussions in Rutba House, *School(s) for Conversion*.

9. See the varied but related examples of Emmaus (www.emmaus.org.uk), Betel (www.betel.org.uk) and Yeldall Manor (www.yeldall.org.uk).

after what we cannot attain. It would be fascinating to study the parallels between addiction recovery and more mainstream discipleship, particularly in terms of fostering honesty, accountability, vulnerability, the recognition of destructive behaviors and thought patterns, and the consequent re-disciplining of the mind (could one say "transforming"?). Once again the poor at the edge of society have a lot to teach us.

When I discuss living together with Christians a regular argument, or fear, is that any such experiment, at any level, will only lead to a "holy huddle." Christians will only withdraw from the world to work on their own spirituality. Basically, it's a cop-out. If it were not so serious this would be hilarious, coming as it often does from a church dwindling in numbers, with no common life to speak of and unable to welcome wounded people like Mark into their midst. That seems a pretty damning picture of selfish spiritual introspection. Mark's story, in fact, shows us the importance of shared houses. A shared house is more than the sum of its parts. It has a greatly increased capacity to welcome needy individuals precisely because there are more people around. The risk of hospitality is shared, as is the burden of need. I do not need to be as afraid about what may happen to my children, or my possessions, or my sanity, because there are other people around to look out for us. We share the frustrations and the joys together. The ancient Christian tradition of hospitality needs to be recovered, with all that this involves.[10] Instead of (in some cases alongside, in some cases replacing) the sterile, structured world of institutional "care" (be it hospitals, hostels, care homes, or prisons) there is a radical Christian alternative of shared houses, shared lives, and shared families. What Mark needed was a wider family, not some money for a bed and breakfast. There are too many people—adults and children—in such desperate need on our doorstep today. We cannot bear these burdens as individual family units; we have to share our homes.

This is never one-way, however. Anyone who has tried to live with anyone else for any period of time can testify to the

10. On this tradition and its reclamation see Pohl, *Making Room*.

frustrations of shared life. It is so annoying that people are so *different*. We have different assumptions of cleanliness, of manners, of discipline, of humor, of noise levels, of spending, of eating and heating and maintenance and . . . life. Jean Vanier, founder of the radically hospitable L'Arche communities[11] that started when he invited two people with Downs Syndrome to live with him, wrote, "While we are alone, we could believe we loved everyone. Now that we are with others, living with them all the time, we realise how incapable we are of loving, how much we deny to others, how closed in on ourselves we are."[12] It is not only the case that "iron sharpens iron" (Prov 27:17) but also that we grow together in love, towards and in Jesus (Eph 4:15–16). Shared life exposes our pettiness and selfishness, our desire to control others and our world, our prejudice and pride. As such it is an invaluable tool of discipleship, as the Spirit breathes new creation over our wounded egos and we get the chance to see what mutual love, service, and honesty look like.[13] In such mundane things as how we leave the toilet, or how we do the dishes, we glimpse the utterly practical and utterly transforming work of God, inviting us to practice "looking to the interests of others" and thus having the mind of the Messiah (Phil 2:4–5).

There are multiple other benefits to shared housing (to any degree). Bills are lessened, freeing people up to explore different ways of working or perhaps just doing a lot less so they can better love and welcome people. We saw how crucial this imaginative approach to life and work is to salvation in chapter 2. Expensive goods such as washing machines and cookers are shared, lessening both economic and environmental burdens and thus embodying a bit more justice. Opportunities for shared food are increased (and shared meals should be central to the praxis of our faith, we who

11. www.larche.org.uk

12. Vanier, *Community and Growth*, 26.

13. Henri Nouwen exemplified and expounded much of this dynamic as he moved from academia to life in a L'Arche community. Among his numerous works see Nouwen, *Return of the Prodigal; Inner Voice; Way of the Heart; Show me the Way; Here and Now.*

participate in our Messiah, as one body, through a shared meal; food is sacred), along with shared prayer. Released from the burden of having to do and organize everything in a household we are liberated to find our particular place and practice our particular gifts, as part of a body. A watching world may laugh, or scorn, or look on bemused, but if such shared life exhibits more justice, peace, and joy then we can be sure that we are stepping closer to the kingdom. Indeed, we may find that as we step away from the idol of the individual (and the subtle temptations of that other "inviolable" idol, the family as defined by blood rather than faith) we are actually part of something greater (Mark 10:28–31). As we share life we find that we have other brothers, sisters, mothers, and even in the midst of difficulties we find eternal life.

The fear that individualism fosters is struck a great blow by these relationships of love. No longer need I be anxious about providing at all times for myself or my family. I have a wider family to call on. It is especially in times of difficulty that we need this extra capacity. Times of bereavement, of unemployment, of illness; times when there's no money, of debt, of struggle; times when we are confronted with the needy stranger, with devastation, with poverty. In all of this we need the sense of security not just in God but in the family of faith that will allow us to face these situations with grace, hope, and joy.

Shared life need not mean a shared roof. As we said, there is a spectrum of shared life and we often need to start small. There a thousand other things we can practice sharing, great and small. The more we do so the more sharing, and the love that it exhibits, becomes a habit of our hearts and lives. Share money, share food, share work. Share prayer, share cars, share time. Share possessions, share debts, share doubt, share joy. Hebrews 13 is full of such sharing, from radical hospitality to radical generosity and liberation from greed, to sharing the faith of those who went before us and praising God. "Do not neglect to do good and share what you have." (Heb 13:16a).

While the individual is an idol in our culture, and while our faith is the faith of a body rather than private persons, we still have individual decisions to make. We are accountable for our individual deeds (2 Cor 5:10). This does not reduce everything ultimately to individual terms. Rather, we must discern our individual place within the wider body seeking the justice and peace of God's kingdom. It would be impossible to even list the areas to be considered, for they are as broad and deep as life itself and will vary from one person to the next (such is the task of discipleship!), but we will consider some important areas as we close.[14]

First, pensions. Or pensions and retirement. If putting aside money so we can live long, comfortable lives into our old age is not "storing up treasures on earth" I'm not sure what is. Jesus' words are unambiguous: we are to give what we have away to the poor and seek God's kingdom (Matt 6:19–21; Luke 12:13–21, 32–34). We saw in the last chapter that the reality of poverty means we cannot justify such savings. It is not good stewardship; it's idolatry that shows us where our hearts lie. It is intimately connected to the concept of retirement, where we must not be a burden on others when we can work no longer. Can you glimpse the lies of the idols? Are people only valued for economic productivity? What sort of family are we if we expect our elders to either provide for themselves or shuffle off to a care home to die? What sort of statement is that about our level of mutual love and concern? While there is breath in our body we "work" for the kingdom and are called to both bless and be blessed by others. If I tend an elderly parent I am acting in love, just as they are by allowing themselves to be thus tended. We build one another up.

Second, banking. It continues to amuse me that Christians who are vehement in their opposition to gambling happily give countless thousands to financial institutions that bet on the stock market, destabilize global financial systems, fund arms companies and environmentally destructive projects, and foster a culture of greed. Where are the Christian financiers advocating for and

14. Foster, *Celebration of Discipline,* has an excellent balance between inward and outward disciplines for the life of the individual and the life of community.

modeling an alternative?[15] Where is the subversive praxis of the church withdrawing her money from such corrupt institutions and storing it instead in the bellies of the poor? Most people in the UK still bank with one of the Big Four—HSBC, Barclays, Lloyds, RBS—but even in a broken financial system there are alternatives. If we're going to hoard money we may as well hoard it in the best possible place.[16]

Third, shopping. We are defined as consumers, with the produce of the world laid before us. It is counter-cultural and liberating to step away from this. Try not spending money on anything other than food or bills for a month, or a year. While actually consuming less is incumbent on Christians (we don't have three planets, remember) we need to be far more discerning about what we do buy. Organic and Fairtrade labels are at least a step towards justice but the wider web of global commerce must be unearthed. There are resources out there to sharpen our thinking and praxis in this complex morass of oppression and injustice of both creation and workers. The wonderful research of groups such as Ethical Consumer[17] is a good place to start.

Fourth, leisure and domestic life. The divide between "public" and "private" life is a false one. Our lives are whole, and laid down for the kingdom as a whole. This means that pursuits traditionally left to individual desires and whims need to be thought-through in terms of the kingdom. It may not be just to fly around the world and snowboard down mountains that cannot sustain such activity. It may not foster peace to have a domestic life ruled by the powerful stories of television or computer games. Spending vast amounts of time and money on a private hobby that brings no beauty or blessing to others may not be an appropriate course of action. We are not legalistic, banning entire areas of general activity (there may be games that foster fellowship and joy in shared hobbies, for example) but we are people of new creation and are called to act as

15. See Relational Tithe, *Economy of Love*.

16. www.moveyourmoney.org.uk

17. www.ethicalconsumer.org. For broader coverage of global issues and justice see the work of New Internationalist, www.newint.org

such. There is much that is degrading in our world; we are called to be salt and light (Matt 5:13–16), not participating in the works of darkness but living joyfully in the light (Eph 5:8–9, in the context of chapters 4–6 as a whole).

In all of these areas, and many more, we see how the individual is an idol and how God invites us to walk in a different way. This is absolutely to do with how we live—from who we share our house with to what we do for leisure—as of fundamental importance if we claim to believe something different from the wider world. The paths to the kingdom are narrow and winding—oft times we cannot see around the next corner, or whether the way ahead is clear of obstacles—but they are paths trodden by a pioneer before us (Heb 12:2) and they lead to a city where all is renewal and there is joy unutterable (Rev 21–22). In the meantime, we walk in step with the Spirit (Gal 5:25).

One of the most challenging examples of a life liberated from possessions and practicing generosity that I have been blessed by is William's. William had spent long years on the streets, often battling with various substances. His life held a great deal of pain and loss that he never really spoke about. He knew what to do to survive on the streets and he was content to do so, always keeping himself as clean and as dry as possible. He spent some months sleeping in my car, along with squats and the drop-in.

In stark contrast to many others in a similar position William had no desire for possessions. He wore his clothes, carried little, and gave away what he had. When two young lads from Romania found themselves homeless on the island it was William who took them under his wing, William who shared his warm clothes and hideaways with them. He always insisted that he could only ever wear one shirt at a time, so why would he want more? There was a settled sense of peace about his decisions, an air of liberation from the literal weight of the things so many of us spend our lives amassing. In this William seemed to embody what has been called a "theology of enough,"[18] content with what he had. He would often speak of the pleasure of sitting and watching some birds feeding, or the hedgehogs who shared the cemetery where he often slept.

I know enough of William, and have had enough experience with others in such circumstances, not to idealize or romanticize such a life. I do not think that we should all live on the streets and sleep with hedgehogs in cemeteries. Yet I do think that we can learn something from those who do. William had a simple, lighthearted approach to life and possessions that reminded me of Jesus' words in Matthew 6. He practiced an open-handed generosity that put my selfish, tight-fisted unwillingness to share what I had to shame. In this at least William participated in the kingdom, and blessed those of us who knew him. In this culture of speed and possessions, of denying others their rights so I can have my luxuries, of insisting that I can live alone and shape my world, we need the simplicity and generosity of the theology of enough that William embodied.

18. Claiborne, "Sharing Economic Resources," 31–32.

Conclusion

The God of Love and the Joy of the Kingdom

> Ho, everyone who thirsts, come to the waters; and you that have no money, come, buy and eat! Come, buy wine and milk without money and without price. Why do you spend your money for that which is not bread, and your labour for that which does not satisfy? Listen carefully to me, and eat what is good, and delight yourselves in rich food . . . For my thoughts are not your thoughts, nor are your ways my ways, says the LORD. For as the heavens are higher than the earth, so are my ways higher than your ways and my thoughts than your thoughts . . . For you shall go out in joy, and be led back in peace; the mountains and the hills before you shall burst into song, and all the trees of the field shall clap their hands . . . Thus says the LORD: Maintain justice, and do what is right, for soon my salvation will come, and my righteousness be revealed.
>
> —ISAIAH 55:1–2, 8–9, 12, 56:1

I consider that the sufferings of this present time are not worth comparing with the glory about to be revealed to us. For the creation waits with eager longing for the revealing of the

children of God; for the creation was subjected to futility, not
of its own will but by the will of the one who subjected it, in
hope that the creation itself will be set free from its bondage
to decay and will obtain the freedom because of the glory of
the children of God. We know that the whole creation has been
groaning in labour pains until now; and not only the creation,
but we ourselves, who have the first fruits of the Spirit, groan
inwardly while we wait for adoption, the redemption of our
bodies. For in hope we were saved.

—ROMANS 8:18–24A

THE VISION OF GOD's kingdom is always a joyous one, and it births
joy in those who glimpse it even in the midst of suffering. Isaiah
dreams of a time when there is a free invitation to the feast of God,
not dependent on wealth. It is a feast that satisfies. A feast of peace
and justice where creation itself bursts into praise for the good
God. That free invitation to such life was found on the lips of Jesus
(John 4:13–14, 6:35). If we partake of the bread and water of life we
do not hunger or thirst again.

Paul, in a climactic passage in his greatest letter, having just
mentioned the church being led out of slavery by the Spirit of God
(Rom 8:12–17), is full of a vision of the glory that awaits God's
children. It is a hope and a glory not of escaping the world (to
"heaven" or elsewhere) but of seeing creation itself released from
bondage, free of decay and flourishing under the loving care of
God's children (cf, Rom 5:17, where those who receive the abundance of grace reign in life through Jesus). This is the hope that
orients the church. This is the hope that leads to joy.

Anyone who has passed through the waters of addiction—be it to
substances, images, or behaviors—can testify to something of the
new life found on the far side of suffering. A new existence after
a sort of death. They can also testify to the hope that led them

through such difficulties. It requires a vision of how life could be following liberation from bondage.

I have experienced something of this dynamic myself. For the best part of a decade growing up I struggled with addictive thought patterns and behaviors. Most of it was a struggle on my own, deceiving myself that the only thing that mattered was sorting it out between me and God. I must have gone through thousands of cycles of serious prayer and repentance, yearning for healing and freedom, and lapsing back into addiction. Looking back I can see how the secrecy only fed the addiction and kept me enslaved, and how complicit I was in that self-deceit.

It was only when I was caught and confronted in my addiction that I began to be serious about getting help. Stopping the behavior was one thing; stopping the thoughts took much longer. It was a long journey of struggle. At times it felt like a death, like something that was an intrinsic part of me was dying, and there was much pain. It hurts to give up something that has so totally consumed your mental and spiritual space. It hurts to give up an idol. At such times it was difficult to remember hope. The idea that I might one day be free of that which had held me seemed unthinkable.

And yet the Spirit that hovered over the waters at creation hovers over broken lives still. On the other side of the cross stands the resurrection. There is a hope and a love that does not fail, and a freedom that this brings. The idols may rage, but they are impotent. There may be pain, but compared to the glory about to be revealed to us it counts as nothing.

The church is a people of the cross and resurrection. We are irrevocably shaped by the death and resurrection of the Messiah. The life, death, and resurrection of Jesus is the foundation of everything else. The death Jesus died only makes sense in the context of the life he lived, a life embodying God's kingdom. The horror of the cross and the absence of God only makes sense in the light of the resurrection. The resurrection only makes sense following such a life and such a death, with Jesus confronting and defeating all powers and ushering in a new time, a new kingdom, a new creation.

This cross-and-resurrection dynamic, in the context of the kingdom, must be borne in mind if the idols we give ourselves to are to be confronted and overthrown. It will not do to pray some prayers, believe in Jesus, and hope that everything will work out all right. That would be to demean the cross that means death and fail to take the reality of the idols seriously. It would leave us in the same state of self-deceit I spent so much time in, praying for freedom but not understanding that something had to die, unwilling to take the hard road to new life. If there is cheap grace, in Bonhoeffer's phrase,[1] then there is also a cheap cross.

Neither must we so obsess with the cross, the suffering, and the death we must undergo that we forget the resurrection. That would leave us crucified and helpless, without God in the world. It would leave us in the state I sometimes lapsed into as I suffered the death of the addiction, refusing to believe that life could be different or that there was a hope of freedom.

In this time and place we are a hurried, harried people. We yearn to have instantaneous accomplishment and consummation. The desire to have it all and to have it now bleeds over into Christian discourse. Effort is derided, perhaps in a latent fear that we might therefore be taking the place of God's work in our lives. Pray the prayers, glance at your Bible, and get on with your life while claiming maturity in Jesus. We race to the resurrection without the cross, and we remain ignorant of the life that led the Messiah there. Paul's repeated discussions of suffering as a key mark of Christian life and witness provoke bafflement (Rom 8:17; 1 Cor 4:8–13; 2 Cor 4–6, 11:21–33; Gal 2:19–21, 5:11, 6:14; Eph 6:10–20; Phil 1:12–30; Col 1:24) and Jesus' words about taking up our crosses (Mark 8:34–35) are relegated to hyperbole. In the world of the Messiah who became a slave the path of obedience is costly (Phil 2:5–11). Faith, hope, and love are not pious fictions or fleeting emotions. They are the hard-won triumphs of those

---

1. Bonhoeffer, *Cost of Discipleship*, 3–4.

who have passed through the waters of baptism and death into a whole new life.

What can sustain this delicate balance of life-cross-resurrection? How do we keep our bearings? In all of this it is the kingdom of God that provides the focus and hope, the kingdom that is often accompanied by suffering and yet results in peace, justice, and joy.

The importance of joy in the present time cannot be overstated. Only people of the cross and resurrection can look on the horror and misery of this broken world and neither despair or turn away but respond in self-giving love. That love demands a joyous vision to sustain it, the life of God renewing and transforming us into our true humanity. Congregations, in all areas of their individual and communal life, need to create contexts of joy. We urgently need contexts of joy in our homes and around our tables, in our jobs and finances, in our services and leisure, in our spending and being spent. Joy demands hope, the hope of the kingdom that one day all things will be put right and the faith that this is already happening in the work of the Spirit in the present. While there is a hard-nosed seriousness about the depth of pain and the suffering that must be undergone in the present there is the joy that is the Spirit's work as we are led into freedom. Christians are people marked by the joy of the kingdom, filled with the fruit of the Spirit as they walk the difficult path deeper into the kingdom of God.

Walking in love, sharing the life of God and loving one another, puts us right back in the world of 1 John. Fellowship with Jesus means walking as he walked, which means a life of practical love. 1 John 4 is perhaps the greatest chapter on love in the NT. Love is from God. We are born of God if we love. Love is seen in the person of Jesus. This is what love looks like. If we love one another with the same love we see God. We abide in him by the Spirit. We love because he first loved us. There is no fear in love. Here we see the heart of the joy and the hope that consumed the early church: the love of God known in lives marked by love. This is why it matters what we do. This love is what undergirds our understanding of freedom and salvation. This love confronts the violence of the state and its rulers, even as it mocks the defeated powers (Col 2:15).

This love does not tolerate poverty or need but responds in self-giving generosity. This love is why we can never stand alone, for love requires someone *to* love. This love is the source of our life and the mark by which we are known (John 13:35).

It is this same love that stands against all the idols. The idols rule by fear, worming their way into our lives and societies and insisting that we cannot do without them. As we give ourselves to their sway we become to believe their lies, the lies we tell ourselves, and we cease to have even the capacity to imagine life differently. When the lies are exposed we are terrified because we think we need the idols. To all of this 1 John 4:18 says "there is no fear in love, but perfect love casts out fear." This is why the church is such a challenge to the idols: she lives the fearless life. Lies have no power over her. She may suffer but she is unafraid. Along with the joy, the hope, and the love the Christian life is the fearless life. Why? Because we have died and we live to God. It is no longer we who live, but the Messiah who lives in us, who loved us and gave himself for us (Gal 2:19–20). Death, the evil that lurks behind all fear, no longer has dominion over us (Rom 6:9).

In the end all words cease. Prophecies fall silent. Ink dries on the page and the books gather dust on the shelves. Arguments are cast aside, futile and unresolved. What remains is love. What remains is the life that we live. The proof and the joy of all our faith and striving are found in the lives we live. But not just our own life. We find that our individual life is bound up in the communal life, in the ecclesial life of the church. And more, we find that our lives are hidden with the Messiah in God (Col 3:3) and that we stand by his life, sharing in his death and participating in the resurrection that has ushered in the new creation.

A kingdom of peace and justice. A creation joyous in its liberation from decay. A joy even in the face of suffering. A hope in the God who raised Jesus from the dead (Rom 4:17, 24). A love that casts out fear and overturns the idols' reign. Here the threads are drawn together into a rich, multicolored tapestry, a vision that we can and must participate in today. This is the way that we walk. People marked by such a vision and way of life are subversive in a world of fear and suspicion, evoking attraction and question as much as hostility and scorn. Now we are God's people, called out of darkness into light, conducting ourselves in such a way that even when we are maligned people see our good deeds and glorify God (1 Pet 2:10–12). The yearning, longing, aching cry that we started with is still the content of our prayer, still the object of our mission, still the motivation for our dancing dreams even as we have the foretaste of the wonderful reality in the touch of the Spirit, the pledge of our inheritance towards redemption (Eph 1:14).

No King but God.

Bibliography

Betel. http://www.betel.org.uk.

Bonhoeffer, Dietrich. *The Cost of Discipleship*. London: SCM, 2001.

———. *Life Together*. London: SCM, 1954.

Brimlow, Robert. "What about Hitler?" In *A Faith Not Worth Fighting For: Addressing Commonly Asked Questions about Christian Nonviolence*, edited by Tripp York and Justin Bronson Barringer, 44–59. Eugene, OR: Cascade, 2012.

The Bruderhof. *Foundations of our Faith and Calling*. New York: Plough, 2012.

———. http://www.bruderhof.com/en.

The Catholic Worker. http://www.catholicworker.org.

Claiborne, Shane. "Mark 2: Sharing Economic Resources with Fellow Community Members and the Needy Among Us." In *School(s) for Conversion: 12 Marks of a New Monasticism*, edited by The Rutba House, 26–38. Eugene, OR: Cascade, 2005.

Claiborne, Shane and Chris Haw. *Jesus for President: Politics for Ordinary Radicals*. Grand Rapids: Zondervan, 2008.

Driver, John. *Images of the Church in Mission*. Scottdale, PA: Herald, 1997.

Ellul, Jacques. *Anarchy and Christianity*. Grand Rapids: Eerdmans, 1991.

———. *The Meaning of the City*. Eugene, OR: Wipf and Stock, 2011.

———. *The Subversion of Christianity*. Eugene, OR: Wipf & Stock, 2001.

Emmaus. http://www.emmaus.org.uk.

Ethical Consumer. http://www.ethicalconsumer.org.

Fiddes, Paul S. *Participating in God: A Pastoral Doctrine of the Trinity*. London: Darton, Longman & Todd, 2000.

Foster, Richard. *Celebration of Discipline: The Path to Spiritual Growth*. London: Hodder & Stoughton, 1999.

Goddard, Andrew. *Living the Word, Resisting the World: The Life and Thought of Jacques Ellul*. Carlisle, UK: Paternoster, 2002.

Graih. http://www.graih.org.im.

Heschel, Abraham J. *The Prophets*. New York: Perennial Classics, 2001.

Horsley, Richard A. *Jesus and Empire: The Kingdom of God and the New World Disorder*. Minneapolis, MN: Fortress, 2003.

————., ed. *Paul and Empire: Religion and Power in Roman Imperial Society.* Harrisburg, PA: Trinity, 1997.

Kreider, Alan, and Eleanor Kreider. *Worship and Mission After Christendom.* Milton Keynes, UK: Paternoster, 2009.

L'Arche. http://www.larche.org.uk.

MacCulloch, Diarmaid. *A History of Christianity: The First Three Thousand Years.* London: Penguin, 2010.

Murray, Stuart. *The Naked Anabaptist: The Bare Essentials of a Radical Faith.* Milton Keynes, UK: Paternoster, 2011.

New Internationalist. http://www.newint.org.

Nouwen, Henri J.M. *Here and Now: Living in the Spirit.* London: Darton, Longman & Todd, 1994.

————. *The Inner Voice of Love: A Journey Through Anguish To Freedom.* London: Darton, Longman & Todd, 1997.

————. *The Return of the Prodigal Son: A Story of Homecoming.* London: Darton, Longman & Todd, 1994.

————. *The Way of the Heart.* London: Darton, Longman & Todd, 1999.

Pohl, Christine D. *Making Room: Recovering Hospitality as a Christian Tradition.* Grand Rapids: Eerdmans, 1999.

Relational Tithe. *Economy of Love.* Kansas City, MO: The House Studio, 2010.

The Rutba House, ed. *School(s) for Conversion: 12 Marks of a New Monasticism.* Eugene, OR: Cascade, 2005.

Schlabach, Gerald W. "Must Christian Pacifists Reject Police Force?" In *A Faith Not Worth Fighting For: Addressing Commonly Asked Questions about Christian Nonviolence,* edited by Tripp York and Justin Bronson Barringer, 60–84. Eugene, OR: Cascade, 2012.

Sider, Ronald J. *Rich Christians in an Age of Hunger: A Biblical Study.* Sevenoaks, UK: Hodder & Stoughton, 1977.

The Simple Way. http://www.thesimpleway.org.

Sobrino, Jon. *Christology at the Crossroads: A Latin American Approach.* Maryknoll, NY: Orbis, 1978.

————. *No Salvation Outside the Poor: Prophetic-Utopian Essays.* Maryknoll, NY: Orbis, 2008.

Stackhouse, Ian. *The Day is Yours: Slow Spirituality in a Fast-Moving World.* Milton Keynes, UK: Paternoster, 2008.

Vanier, Jean. *Community and Growth.* Mahwah, NJ: Paulist, 1989.

Williamson, Mabel. *"Have We No Right?"* London: China Inland Mission, 1958.

Wright, Christopher J.H. *The Mission of God: Unlocking the Bible's Grand Narrative.* Downers Grove, IL: IVP Academic, 2006.

————. *The Mission of God's People: A Biblical Theology of the Church's Mission.* Grand Rapids: Zondervan, 2010.

Wright, N.T. *Jesus and the Victory of God.* Christian Origins and the Question of God 2. London: SPCK, 1996.

————. *Justification: God's Plan and Paul's Vision.* London: SPCK, 2009.

————. *The New Testament and the People of God.* Christian Origins and the Question of God 1. London: SPCK, 1992.

————. *Paul and the Faithfulness of God.* 2 vols. Christian Origins and the Question of God 4. London: SPCK, 2013.

————. *The Resurrection of the Son of God.* Christian Origins and the Question of God 3. London: SPCK, 2003.

Yeldall Manor. http://www.yeldall.org.uk.

www.ingramcontent.com/pod-product-compliance
Lightning Source LLC
Chambersburg PA
CBHW071835090426
42737CB00012B/2249